Alexandra Bircken
Rektusdiastase

Bonner Kunstverein
Kunstverein in Hamburg

Verlag der Buchhandlung
Walther König

LEARNING
RESOURCES
CENTRE

Inhalt CONTENTS

Wie kommt der Fisch ins Band? [1]

Der Mensch ist in der Welt ein bewegliches Element: Er handelt schnell, erfindet, macht und tut, markiert sich Räume und Orte. Dagegen oder vielmehr mit ihm existiert das, was dauert. Er ist als Wesen tendenziell ephemer, baut sich Nester hier und dort, schmiegt sich an Waldeshänge oder Senken wie der Vogel an den Ast. Das, was er baut, mag ihn überdauern, fällt aber zu irgendeinem Zeitpunkt dem „zän" (dem „kainos", dem Neuen) zum Opfer. Was durchaus auch sinnig ist, da der Mensch sich schneller bewegt als eine Wanderdüne, von hier nach dort reist und sich zeitweise der Energien bemächtigt, die um ihn herrschen.

Dass gefundene Objekte, natürlicher wie nicht natürlicher Art, gesammelt, genommen und in Kunstwerken mehr oder weniger verarbeitet werden (können): ein Gemeinplatz. Dass sie dabei Spuren ihrer vorherigen Zusammenhänge in sich tragen: auch ein Gemeinplatz. Upcycling statt Downcycling kennt die Kunst schon lange.

Dass dabei ein Dialog zwischen dem Künstler, dem Verarbeiter, und dem Gegebenen/Gefundenen/Gesuchten entsteht: vermutlich auch ein Gemeinplatz. Aus den (wieder aufgelebten) aktuellen Diskussionen heraus über ein Revival des Begriffs des Anthropozäns, mit dem schon einmal um die Gunst der Menschheit (oder eher der Geologen?) gebuhlt wurde[2] und der möglicherweise die Idee des Holozäns[3] ablösen könnte, ist dieser aber evtl. nicht ganz unwesentlich. Interessant daran ist die Rezeption auch innerhalb eines künstlerischen, d.h. nicht fachspezifischen Kontextes. Schon geht es um Fragen nach der Bedeutung dieser Veränderung für die kuratorische Praxis in naturorientierten wie auch anderen Museen.[4] Eine eigentlich sehr nahe liegende Entwicklung, da der Mensch also nun in die Weltgeschichte eingehen kann, in die „longue durée"[5] mit seinem „Anthro-" einfällt. Holozän klingt da noch ganz anders. Der Begriff erzählt von einer Art allumfassendem Gleichgewicht, wenn man das „zän", das Neue, einmal abspaltet. Jetzt also der Mensch und seine Einflüsse. Unleugbar sind diese sicherlich; Anthropozän, das menschlich (gemachte) Neue. Alles neu macht der Mai, jetzt: Alles neu macht der Mensch.

Damit steht diese wissenschaftliche Verschiebung im Kontext der menschlichen Evolution. Er unterscheidet sich von anderen Lebewesen durch seine Fähigkeiten, gezielt und in der Gemeinschaft die Welt zu bearbeiten, die Natur und ihre Vorgänge nutzbar zu machen, Werkzeuge und Techniken zu entwickeln, die auf zukünftige Lebensbedingungen und Erfolge angelegt sind. Das menschliche Dasein ist also seit tausenden von Jahren darauf angelegt, sich von der Natur abzugrenzen, indem es ein Überlegenheitsmoment ins Spiel bringt.

Der Transfer des Anthropozänbegriffs aus dem geologischen in einen kulturgeschichtlichen Kontext verzerrt das Bild ein wenig, wenn der Mensch als sich selbst historisierendes Wesen den Wert der und des Anderen aus dem Blick verliert und aus der Langzeitperspektive in den Fokussiermodus wechselt. Der Blick auf temporäre Errungenschaften tendiert dazu, das Vergehen und das Werden, das Sich-Etwas-Zunutze-Machen und die Wertigkeiten, die darin aufscheinen und verschwinden, zu übersehen.

Umgekehrt ist das Aufscheinen einer Idee von Dauer ein Aspekt, der größere Zusammenhänge und Beziehungen zwischen dem Menschen und seiner Umwelt hervortreten lässt und damit einen ethischen Standpunkt implizieren kann. Was sich ganz gut mit dem Konkurrenzbegriff Noosphäre trifft, der, von griechisch „nous" für Geist/Verstand, weniger das Handeln des Menschen in den Vordergrund stellt, als philosophisch argumentiert.[6]

Ein Ast, Blätter, Stroh, der Gummiabrieb eines Reifens, eine Resopalplatte, ein Schaukelpferd – all dies ist Seiendes. Manche der Materialien in Alexandra Birckens Werk sind natürlicher Art, einige sind vom Menschen hergestellt, aber alle haben zunächst einmal keinen besonderen Wert mehr. Es mag ihn einmal gegeben haben, aber in der Zwischenzeit sind sie Reststücke geworden. Nun, nach ihrem Ausscheiden aus der Determination des Konsums, in der neuen Kontextlosigkeit und ohne funktionale Bindungen, stehen die gemachten Dinge zu einer freien Verfügung, können gefunden und gesammelt werden. Abgeworfen vom Menschen oder von Bäumen. Aus ihren ursprünglichen Funktionszusammenhängen befreit, bringen natürliche Dinge weder neue Früchte noch Fortpflanzung hervor, sind Warengüter nicht mehr zum Tausch und damit zum Konsum und zum Hervorbringen neuen Kapitals geeignet. In dieser Freiheit können sie stattdessen andere, ihnen innewohnende Energien und Möglichkeiten entfalten, lassen zum Vorschein kommen, was keinem Fortschritt im kapitalistischen Sinne verpflichtet ist. Der Fortschritt ist dementsprechend ein anderer: der einer reinen Nutzbarkeit[7] und damit einer existenzialistischen Performance.

Diese Aspekte beziehen sich auf die einzelnen Elemente als zur Verfügung stehendes Material. Indem Alexandra Bircken aus ihnen Skulpturen macht, die in fertiger Form in einen neuen Kreislauf, die Entwicklungen symbolischer wie materieller Art und das Kapital des Kunstmarktes, eingespeist werden, fügen sie sich nichtsdestotrotz ihrerseits in ein Verwertungssystem ein.

Dass der Mensch der Welt nun auch auf geologischer Ebene seinen Stempel aufdrückt, liegt vor allen Dingen an Prinzipien der Nutzbarmachung mit dem Ziel weiterer Nutzbarmachung und vorwiegend materieller Entfaltung. Die Objekte und die in ihnen niedergelassenen Dinge von Alexandra Bircken sind im Gegenzug dazu das, was man im Englischen wohl mit „humble" – etwas wie bescheiden oder zurückhaltend – beschreiben würde. Ihre momentane Ruhe löst sich von Verwendungszwecken und wendet der Selbständigkeit der Dinge den Blick zu, der sich nur jenseits von Konsum und Verlangen entwickeln kann. Damit kann der Ast genuin konstruktives Element eines Gebildes werden, die Jacke eine schützende Membran, die Strumpfhose eine Haut, ohne dass sie Zwecken unterworfen wären, die über diese grundlegenden Eigenschaften hinausgehen würden. In der Zeitlosigkeit des Kunstwerks – betrachtet man es in Relation zu schnell zirkulierenden Waren – entsteht eine Dauerhaftigkeit und Wertigkeit der Dinge. Damit werden sie wieder für die Arbeit gewonnen. Insofern kommt es zu einer Reanimation ihrer Herstellungsbedingungen entgegen ihrer Fetischisierung als Ware oder der Ästhetisierung als Kunstobjekt.[8] Da es sich bei den Werken von Alexandra Bircken im strikt Duchampschen Diktum de facto nicht um Readymades handelt – es sind weder „unaltered" noch „assisted", weder „rectified" noch „reciprocal" Readymades – kann auch nicht von einer Ästhetisierung als Kunstobjekt die Rede sein. Die mit dem Aufrufen der Bedingungen ihrer Entstehung einhergehende Form der Unmittelbarkeit und der Bezug zum menschlichen Handeln, dort wo es dringlich ist oder erscheint, reaktiviert ein nicht-entfremdetes Verhältnis, bzw. stellt sich der Entfremdung entgegen.

Der Mensch ist Mensch im Sinne eines fähigen und von der Natur abgegrenzten Wesens geworden, wo er sich gegen sie zu schützen und sie zu nutzen vermag. Auf diesem Grenzbereich von Abhängigkeit und Unterwerfung, den beständigen Neuverhandlungen dieses Abgrenzungsprozesses, platzieren sich die Skulpturen von Alexandra Bircken in einem Schwebezustand, was die Aufmerksamkeit für die (Be)Arbeit(ung) und die Zeitlichkeit, die Verletzlichkeit und die Fähigkeit zum Aufbau vielleicht zu lenken vermag.

Hieran schließt sich die Frage nach Formen der Gewalt oder Brutalität an: Wer bemächtigt sich wessen, und wessen Integrität wird dabei gestört? Oder gibt es so etwas wie faire Koexistenz? Obwohl es sich, wie oben angemerkt, bei den Werken nicht um klassische Readymades handelt, verwendet Alexandra Bircken ihre gefundenen Dinge und Objekte im Prinzip als Readymades. Jedes bleibt sich im Wesentlichen treu, wird nicht verändert, sondern in einer überschreibenden Weise inkorporiert. Es sind Zusammenfügungen und Zusammenschlüsse, denen verwebende und Halt gebende Materialien eine skulpturale Form verleihen. Damit werden sie zwar erneut gebraucht (im doppelten Sinne eines Nutzens und einer Notwendigkeit), bleiben sich aber im oben angesprochenen und damit wiederum doppelten Sinne treu: unverändert wird etwas eingewebt und erfüllt im Ganzen eine Aufgabe, die grundsätzlich in ihm angelegt ist (z. B. eine Jacke, die Teil der schützenden Außenhaut einer temporären Behausung wird, oder die Wolle, die als Netz eine Zwischenebene einzieht, etwas umspinnt und einen Raum definiert.) Fraglich bleibt, welche Art von Raum hier definiert wird.

Die Herkunft der gefundenen, gesammelten und zusammengesuchten Dinge liegt weitgehend im unmittelbaren, teils im häuslichen Umfeld, ist aber über-narrativ. Damit kommt ihnen kein notwendig symbolischer oder allegorischer Gehalt zu, der im Sinne feministischer Kunst in ihren Anfängen vom Eingebundensein des Künstlersubjektes in seine Zusammenhänge, weiblichen Spezifika und daran geknüpfte gesellschaftliche Trennlinien erzählt.[9] In ihrem häuslichen Kontext berichten die Dinge vielmehr von Besitz im Sinne von Notwendigkeiten; die gesellschaftlichen Konnotationen laufen entsprechend im Subtext mit, verlieren aber gegenüber den konstruktiven Momenten an Bedeutung. Auch das Stricken, Häkeln und Weben erscheint im Werk von Alexandra Bircken als konstruierendes und damit bauendes Element. Es entsteht eine Spannung zwischen der herstellenden, sichtbar tätigen Hand und dem Gebrauch vorhandenen Materials. Im Falle der Warengüter handelt es sich um reproduzierbare Dinge, die industriell gefertigt wurden und als solche unmittelbar erkennbar bleiben. Darin sind sich Tasche, Badewanne, Schaukelpferd, Schlitten und Stofftier alle gleich, auch wenn sie an sich von einander verschieden sind. Aber auch Ast, Blätter, Stroh usw., also die natürlichen Dinge, bleiben in sich erkennbar und betreiben keine Form der Mimikry. Sie lassen sich auch im Werk nicht korrumpieren oder subsumieren. In diese Richtung gibt es keinerlei Versuche; einzig Stabilisierung und Konservierung sind Mittel, die zum Einsatz kommen. Dabei wird ihnen eine Haut übergezogen, z. B. in Form von Kupfer oder einem Bronzeabguss, der erinnernd aufschreibt und damit die alte Bedeutung der Membran als Pergament aufscheinen lässt. Diese Form der Notation kann beinahe mythischen Charakter annehmen und damit größere Bedeutungszusammenhänge zu Tage treten lassen als die engen Bahnen des Warenkreislaufs. In dem Zusammenbringen einzelner Elemente entstehen weniger Zwischenräume als Energieströme und damit Verbindungen und Transformationsprozesse, die in den Materialien angelegt sind und ganz in Ruhe ihre potenzielle Macht entfalten können.

Lebt das Objekt des Konsums im Jetzt, arbeitet Alexandra Bircken einer Vergänglichkeit entgegen und speist ihre Materialien damit in eine neue Form der Nutzbarkeit ein, die danach trachtet, den noch stets erhaltenen Wert zum Vorschein kommen zu lassen. Voraussetzung hierfür ist eine Flexibilität in der Arbeit – als produktive Tätigkeit, nicht im Sinne von Werk, wobei auch ihm diese potenziell zukommt –, die, statt immer gleicher Arbeit, andere Gebrauchsformen integrativer Art findet. Dass sie dabei wieder der Vergänglichkeit anheim fallen, aufgebraucht und aufgelöst werden, ist eine Gefahr oder, positiv gesprochen, Möglichkeit, die erhalten bleibt. Und in diesem Gebrauchswert tief drin steckt der Dialog zwischen Mensch und Material/Ding, der der Tendenz zum Nichts in der wissenschaftlich-technischen Vernunft entgegensteht.[10] Lebt das konsumierte Objekt nur im Verhältnis zu seinem Konsumenten, ist das Ding von anderer Natur: „Die Dinge sind für uns [...] Manifestationen in der Zeit und im Raum"[11].

Um auf die Frage nach dem Raum bei Alexandra Bircken zurückzukommen, gilt es, sich der Spannung zwischen den dynamischen Konzeptionen und dem ihnen zugleich eigenen, latent unbeholfenen Stillstand anzunähern. Der Raum ist dabei einerseits als konkrete Raumbildung in Form von potenziellen Behausungen, als Nester, Hütten, „Baumhäuser", korbartige Aufbauten auf mobilen Einheiten und als Fortbewegungsmittel usw., präsent und andererseits in Form eines häuslichen Referenzsystems. Im ersten Fall beinhaltet das Temporäre und das Nomadische trotz des Vorhandenseins von Dingen eine Form der Loslösung von materiellen Gebundenheiten; Besitz, Nutzbarmachung und Anhäufung lösen sich tendenziell auf. Nichtsdestotrotz bedeutet es, sich vorübergehend häuslich zu machen, dennoch etwas zu besitzen, was sich in einem relativ rudimentären Sein zusammenkauert. Und dieses Rudimentäre bedeutet zugleich, dem, womit und worin man sich niederlässt, eine Form des Eigenlebens zuzugestehen und die Trennung in das handelnde Selbst und das (vollständig) bearbeitete Andere aufzugeben, um den Abstand, der in Konsum und Wissenschaft negiert wird, auf den Plan zu rufen. Erst durch das Niederlassen wird der Ort als Raum erfahrbar, der Raum aber ruft seinerseits das Niederlassen auf den Plan. Das Dasein ist für Heidegger ein Da-Sein, so dass er die menschliche Existenz unmittelbar an das Wohnen bindet; es meint die „Weise, nach der wir Menschen auf der Erde sind"[12] und zwar in einer Weise, die einrichtet und errichtet. In seiner Rückbindung an eine Handlung wird der Raum als dynamische Einheit begriffen, die sich erst in eben dieser Handlung entfaltet[13], womit man wieder zu einer Form von Arbeit zurückgekehrt wäre, im Speziellen einer des Plastischen in der Kunst[14]. Mit ihr, bzw. sie „ist Raum, räumt den Raum ein, enthüllt Raum, bietet die Möglichkeit des ‚Verweilens'".[15] Und dann gehen Kultur und Natur, Arbeit und Raum Hand in Hand.

1: Dieser Titel ist einem Aufsatz aus einem Jahrbuch zur experimentellen Archäologie entlehnt und geht auf ein Missverständnis meinerseits zurück, weshalb ich den Text überhaupt nur gelesen habe. Nichtsdestotrotz ist die Frage, wie der Fisch ins Band kommt, eventuell interessant: sei es als realer Fisch in wasserwirtschaftlicher Bearbeitung oder als gewebter Fisch in einem Gürtel, wie es der Fall im gelesenen Aufsatz war. Grundlegend für das Verständnis der Fischfrage ist in beiden Fällen die Technik.

2: Der Begriff des Anthropozäns wird seit etwa zehn Jahren vermehrt diskutiert. Der Vorschlag zur Einführung stammt von Chemie-Nobelpreisträger Paul Crutzen, der 2002 in dem „Nature"-Artikel „The Geology of Mankind" den bereits aus dem 19. Jahrhundert stammenden Begriff wieder aufnahm. Stratigraphen meinen, der Mensch habe die Erde in den letzten 100 bis 200 Jahren derart stark verändert, dass wir nun in eine neue Epoche einträten.

3: Die Periode des Känozoikums, der Erdneuzeit, begann vor ca. 65 Millionen Jahren. Sie umfasst mehrere Epochen, deren jüngste bis dato das Holozän ist, das ca. 9000 Jahre vor Christus begann.

4: Vgl. das Langzeitprojekt zu genanntem Thema im Haus der Kulturen der Welt in Berlin 2013/2014.

5: „Longue durée" ist ein auf den französischen Historiker Fernand Braudel zurückgehender Begriff, der längere Zeiträume in die Geschichtswissenschaft einführte. Braudel legt allen anderen Zeitebenen und damit auch der Ereignisgeschichte weitgehend gleichbleibende oder sich nur sehr langsam verändernde Strukturen zugrunde (gesellschaftlicher, politischer, wirtschaftlicher und geologischer Art), die als Voraussetzungen für jegliche Geschehnisse gelten.

6: Der Begriff der Noosphäre wurde in den 1920er Jahren vor allem von Teilhard de Chardin und Vladimir Iwanowitsch Vernadskij ausformuliert und ergänzt die Geosphäre und die Biosphäre um eben jene Noosphäre: eine Schicht des Denkens, die alle anderen Sphären umhüllt. Dabei gehen beide von einer Evolution zum Denken hin aus, die allerdings nicht losgelöst von der Materie existiert, sondern an diese gebunden ist. Insofern handelt es sich nach de Chardin bei der Noosphäre um eine Schicht menschlichen Denkens und ihrer Resultate. Bei beiden nimmt die Noosphäre latent heilsgeschichtliche Züge an, geht aber in jedem Fall über ein Erfassen von Tatsachen hinaus. Aktuell scheint der Begriff allerdings nicht von besonders großem Interesse zu sein.

7: Die reine Nutzbarkeit meint eine befreite Nutzbarkeit, die über die bloße Nutzbarkeit im Sinne einer Verwertungslogik hinausgeht.

8: Vgl. John Roberts: The Intangibilities of Form. Skill and Deskilling in Art After the Readymade, London/New York 2007, S. 66.

9: Alexandra Bircken verwendet ein Schaukelpferd ihrer Tochter, dem diese entwachsen ist und es insofern nicht mehr braucht, ohne dass es bedeutsam wäre, dass es sich um das Schaukelpferd eben dieser Tochter handelt. Mary Kellys *Post-Partum Document,* 1973–1979, thematisiert das eigene Erleben im Aufwachsen ihres Kindes mit qualitativ ähnlichen Readymades. Hier ist es unabdingbar, dass es sich um Dinge ihres Sohnes oder aus dem eigenen Umfeld handelt, um die Beziehungsgeflechte und ihre Arbeit innerhalb dieses Prozesses zu thematisieren.

10: Vgl. Dirk-Michael Hennrich: „Das *Ding* im Werk von Vilém Flusser und Eudoro de Sousa", in: Flusser Studies 11, www.flusserstudies.net/pag/11/hennrich-das-ding.pdf, S. 2, letzter Zugriff: 5.12.12.

11: Hennrich, a.a.O., S. 4.

12: Martin Heidegger: „Bauen, Wohnen, Denken", in: ders.: Vorträge und Aufsätze, Stuttgart 1994, S. 141.

13: Vgl. Julia Burbulla: „Heideggers Schweigen. Die philosophische Raumkunst in ihrer Relevanz für die Kunst der Nachkriegszeit", in: kunsttexte.de, 2/2011, www.kunsttexte.de/index.php?id=711&idartikel=38942&ausgabe=38941&zu=491&L=0, S. 2, letzter Zugriff: 26.11.12.

14: Bearbeitet von Heidegger in: Die Kunst und der Raum, St. Gallen 1969.

15: Julia Burbulla: „Heideggers Schweigen", in: kunsttexte.de, 2/2011, S. 6.

Man represents a versatile element in the world: he acts quickly, he is inventive, he busies himself, he marks out his territories and spaces. By contrast, things that last exist in opposition to him, or should we say rather, they coexist. As a species, man tends to be ephemeral, constructing nests here and there, clinging to forested slopes or hollows, like a bird to a branch. The things that he builds may well outlast him, but at some point they too must succumb to the "cene" (the "kainos", the new), which is in itself thoroughly reasonable, as man moves more quickly than a drifting sand dune and travels from here to there and, for a time at least, is able to harness the energies that reign around him.

The fact that found objects, both naturally and unnaturally occurring, can be collected, taken and more or less processed into artworks: a commonplace. The fact that they bear traces of their former context within them: also a commonplace. Art has long since been familiar with upcycling instead of downcycling.
The fact that a dialogue is initiated between the artist, the agent of this processing, and the given/found/searched for object: presumably a commonplace, too. This is perhaps a not insignificant observation judging by the recent reanimated debate about the revival of the term anthropocene, which has already been used[2] to court the favour of mankind (or was it rather the geologists?) and could possibly replace the idea of the Holocene.[3] What is interesting here is its reception within an artistic, that is to say, a non-specialist context. There is already talk about the meaning of this change for curatorial practice in the natural history museum as well as in other institutions.[4] It is actually a more obvious development as man can now finally enter into world history, into the "longue durée",[5] with his very own "anthro" prefix. Holocene has an entirely different ring to it. The term posits a kind of all-embracing equilibrium, if one splits off the aspect of the new implicit in the suffix "cene". And so now, we have man and his influences. Indeed, they are undeniable: anthropocene, the man-made new.
Thus, this scientific shift is situated in the context of human evolution. Man differentiates himself from other life forms through his abilities to process the world in a targeted fashion and in society, to make use of nature and its processes, to develop tools and techniques which are geared towards future conditions for life and achievements. Human existence has been geared for thousands of years towards a demarcation with nature, by introducing a moment of superiority into the proceedings.
The transference of the term anthropocene from the geological into a cultural-historical context distorts the picture to a certain extent when man, as a self-historicising being, loses sight of the value of the Other and switches from a long-term perspective to a narrower "focus mode". The view of temporary achievements reveals a tendency to overlook decay and emergence, the making-use-of-something and the values which appear and disappear within them. Conversely, the emergence of an idea of permanence is an aspect which allows some-what broader contexts and relationships between man and his environment to come to the fore, and thus have the power to imply an ethical standpoint. This coincides well with a competing term, namely the noosphere, which, derived from the Greek "noos" for spirit/reason, focuses less on the actions of man at the forefront of its consideration and more on putting forward a philosophical argument.[6]

A branch, some leaves, straw, the rubber imprint of a tyre, a Formica worktop, a rocking horse, all are "Seiendes" – that which exists. Many of the materials in Alexandra Bircken's work are of natural provenance, some are man-made, but all of them are devoid of any particular value in the first instance. They may well once have had some intrinsic worth, but in the meantime they have just become discarded remnants. So now that they have been excluded from the exigencies of consumption, now that they reside in a new state devoid of context without any functional connection, these made objects or things are freely disposable, they can be found and collected. Discarded by man or by trees. Liberated from their original functional contexts, natural phenomena neither bear new fruit nor possess the possibility of reproduction, they are commodities ill-suited

9

to exchange and thus to consumption and the production of new capital. In this liberated state, they can instead develop different inherent energies and possibilities, which are not obliged to yield progress in the capitalist sense. Progress is consequently a different entity: namely that of pure utility[7] and thereby an existential performance.

These aspects relate to the individual elements as disposable material. By virtue of the fact that Alexandra Bircken turns them into sculptures that are, when finished, absorbed into a new circulation – namely symbolic and material development and the capital of the art market – they nevertheless cohere to a system of utility.

The fact that man is also leaving his imprint on the world on a geological level concerns principles of utilisation with the aim of further utilisation and, above all, material development. Alexandra Bircken's objects and the things that dwell inside them are, by comparison, what one might describe as humble. Their momentary calm releases them from their utility function and turns its attention to the independence of things, which can only develop beyond the world of consumption and desire. In this way, the branch can be a genuinely constructive element in a structure, the jacket can be a protective membrane, nylon stockings can be skin, without any of them being subject to functions that might transcend these fundamental qualities. The timelessness of the artwork – if one views it in relation to the relatively short shelf life of commodities – engenders a permanence and value for things. In this way, they are reclaimed for "work" once more. Thus, we arrive at a reanimation of the conditions of their original production as opposed to their fetishisation as commodities or their aestheticisation as art objects.[8] In the case of Alexandra Bircken's works, we are de facto not talking about readymades in a strictly Duchampian sense – they are neither "unaltered", "assisted", "rectified" nor "reciprocal" ready-mades – but by the same token, it cannot be the case that we are dealing with their aestheticisation as art objects. Their immediate form, which evokes the conditions of their production and the reference to human activity, wherever it is or seems to be a matter of urgency, reactivates a non-alienated relationship, that is to say, it squares up to alienation.

Man has become man in the sense of a capable being clearly distinct from nature, able to protect himself from it, and at the same time, to make use of it. Alexandra Bircken's sculptures situate themselves in a state of stasis in these borderlands of dependence and subjection and the continual renegotiation of this process of demarcation, which is able perhaps to channel our attention to (re)work(ing) and temporality, vulnerability and the capacity for construction.

The question regarding forms of violence or brutality is germane here: who is exerting power over whom and whose integrity is hereby being disrupted? Or is there such a thing as a fair coexistence? Although we are not dealing with classical readymades in these works as mentioned hitherto, Alexandra Bircken does indeed use found things and objects very much as readymades. Every object remains true to its essence, it isn't altered, but instead incorporated in a palimpsestic manner. Conflations, additions and combinations of this kind are lent sculptural form and substance by these interwoven materials. In this way, they are indeed being reused [the German past participle "gebraucht" contains a double sense of "used" and "needed"– The translator], but they remain true to their aforementioned essence and with a double sense: something is interwoven which is unaltered and yet fulfils a function within the whole, which is itself intrinsic (for example, a jacket which becomes part of the protective outer skin of a temporary shelter, or wool which, as a net, introduces an interstitial level, or is woven around something or indeed defines a space). It is questionable which kind of space is being defined here.

The immediate, partly domestic, environment provides the primary origin of found, collected and resourced objects, but is nonetheless supranarrative. In this way, the objects do not necessarily accrue any symbolic or allegorical content, which might impart something – in terms of feminist art in its infancy – about the incorporation of the artist as the subject in her personal connections, specific female attributes and concomitant social dividing lines.[9] In their domestic context, things divulge more about ownership in the sense of necessities;

social connotations reverberate correspondingly within the subtext, but forfeit meaning when confronted with constructional moments. Knitting, crocheting and weaving also feature in Alexandra Bircken's work as constitutive and thereby constructional elements. A tension arises between a productive, visibly active pair of hands and the use of existing materials. In the case of commodities, we are dealing with reproducible objects that have been industrially manufactured and, as such, can be immediately identified. Bags, bathtubs, a rocking horse, a sledge and cuddly toys are all equal, even if they differ from one another. But so too are branches, leaves, straw and so on – that is to say natural things which remain recognisable and do not indulge in any form of mimicry. They do not allow themselves to be corrupted in the work. There are no experiments of any sort in this direction; stabilisation and conservation are the only means deployed here. In so doing, they are coated with a skin, for example, in the form of a copper or bronze cast, which records for posterity, thereby highlighting the ancient meaning of the membrane as parchment. This form of notation can assume almost a mythical character and thus allow contexts of meaning to emerge which are more broad than the narrow channels of commodity circulation. In the compilation of individual elements, it is not primarily interstitial spaces that emerge, but currents of energy and thereby processes of transformation, which are inherent in the materials and can develop their potential power in their own time and way.

If the object of our consumption thrives in the here and now, Alexandra Bircken's work oppugns ephemerality and injects a new type of utility value into her materials that steadfastly displays its perpetually retained, essential value. The precondition here is a flexibility in the working process – as a productive activity, not in the sense of work which, for its part, might potentially derive benefit here – but which is able to find other integrative forms of use rather than a series of repetitive actions. The fact that they might be susceptible once more to ephemerality, used up and dissolved, is a danger, or to put it positively, also an abiding possibility. And deep within this utility value resides the dialogue between man and material/things, which opposes the tendency towards nothingness at the heart of materialist, scientific, technical reason.[10] If the consumed object can only exist in relation to its consumer, then the thing per se has a different nature, "for us, things are […] manifestations in time and in space".[11]

To return to the question of space in the work of Alexandra Bircken, it is necessary to approach the tension between the dynamic conceptions and their own, simultaneously latent, awkward stasis. On the one hand, space is always present as a concrete spatial formation in the shape of potential dwellings, such as nests, huts, "tree houses", basket-like constructions on mobile units and as a means of transport, etc., and on the other, in the form of a domestic system of reference. In the first case, temporariness and the nomadic per se, despite the presence of things, contain a form of release from material ties; property, use and accumulation tend to fall away. Be that as it may, it still means that in dwelling temporarily, one must still own something which engenders a relatively rudimentary existence. At the same time, this rudimentary element means, to a certain extent at least, a life of its own is granted to the thing with and in which one dwells and the separation between the acting Self and the (completely) adapted Other is renounced, in order to invoke the distance which is negated in consumption and science. Only after dwelling is it possible to experience the place as a space, but the space for its part invokes the need for dwelling. For Heidegger, existence ("Dasein") is also a sense of being there ("Da-sein"), with the effect that human existence is immediately connected to dwelling, in the sense of "the way we humans inhabit the earth",[12] indeed, a way that both furnishes and constructs. In its retrospective connection to an action, space is perceived as a dynamic unit, which can only develop in the first instance within this activity,[13] whereby one might arrive at a form of work once more, specifically speaking, at sculpture within art.[14] Thus, sculpture is "space [that] in preserving and opening a region, holds something free gathered around it which grants the possibility of 'tarrying'".[15] And at this point, culture and nature go hand in hand.

1: This title has been borrowed from a yearbook of experimental archaeology and is based on a misunderstanding on my part, which led me to read the text in the first place. Nevertheless, this question is possibly an interesting one: be it a real fish that is being processed within a water management system or a woven fish in a bordure, as was the case in the essay in question. In both cases, technology is of fundamental importance for an understanding of the fish question.

2: The term anthropocene has been widely discussed over the past ten years. The suggestion to introduce it into the nomenclature came from the Nobel Prize-winning atmospheric chemist, Paul Crutzen, who readopted the nineteenth-century concept in an article in *Nature* entitled "The Geology of Mankind" in 2002. Stratigraphers believe that man has had such a significant influence on the world over the past two centuries to constitute a new geological epoch for its lithosphere.

3: The Cenozoic era began 65 million years ago. It encompasses many epochs, the youngest being the Holocene, which began circa 9000 BC.

4: Cf. the long-term project on the topic at the Haus der Kulturen der Welt in Berlin, 2013/2014.

5: "Longue durée" is a term which can be traced back to the French historian Fernand Braudel, which introduced long spans of time into the science of history. Braudel takes largely stable, unchanging structures or at least ones that change gradually (social, political, economic or geological) as the basis for all periods of time and thus the history of events which are the preconditions for all manner of activity.

6: The concept of a noosphere was developed in the 1920s, above all by Pierre Teilhard de Chardin and Vladimir Iwanowitsch Vernadskij in lexical analogy to the geosphere and the biosphere. The noosphere is a layer of thought which envelops all other spheres. Both philosophers proceed from the basis of an evolution towards cognition, but at no time independent of matter or the material world. Thus, according to Teilhard, the noosphere is a layer of human thought and its concomitants. The noosphere contains latent characteristics of the history of salvation in the work of both men, but definitely transcends the mere cataloguing of facts. However, the term doesn't appear to enjoy widespread currency today.

7: Pure utility implies a liberated utility which transcends mere utility in terms of the logics of further processing ("Verwertungslogik").

8: Cf. John Roberts, *The Intangibilities of Form. Skill and Deskilling in Art After the Readymade* (London/New York, 2007), p. 66.

9: Alexandra Bircken uses a rocking horse which her daughter had grown out of and thus no longer needed, without it being significant that it was specifically her daughter's rocking horse. Mary Kelly's *Post-Partum Document*, 1973–1979, focuses thematically upon her own experience in raising her son with qualitatively similar readymades. It is essential in this context that the objects are from her domestic environment or belong to her son, in order to provide the thematic focus for this network of relationships and her work within this process.

10: Cf. Dirk-Michael Hennrich, "Das *Ding* im Werk von Vilém Flusser und Eudoro de Sousa", in: *Flusser Studies*, 11, www.flusserstudies.net/pag/11/hennrich-das-ding.pdf, p. 2 (last accessed: 5.12.12).

11: Hennrich, loc. cit., p. 4.

12: Martin Heidegger, "Bauen, Wohnen, Denken", in: id., *Vorträge und Aufsätze* (Stuttgart, 1994), p. 141.

13: Cf. Julia Burbulla, "Heideggers Schweigen. Die philosophische Raumkunst in ihrer Relevanz für die Kunst der Nachkriegszeit", in: *kunsttexte.de*, 2/2011, www.kunsttexte.de/index.php?id=711&idartikel=38942&ausgabe=38941&zu=491&L=0, p. 2 (last accessed: 26.11.12).

14: Cf. Heidegger, *Die Kunst und der Raum* (St. Gallen, 1969).

15: Julia Burbulla, "Heideggers Schweigen", in: *kunsttexte.de*, 2/2011, p. 6.

Das ‚Resopal'-Möbel oder Die Sinne nehmen nicht einfach die Dinge auf, sondern in ihnen auch eine Form an: Jedes gegenständliche Design ist immer auch ein Design der Sinnlichkeit

(Das unter der Markenbezeichnung ‚Resopal' gehandelte, zur Beschichtung von Oberflächen eingesetzte Kunststoffmaterial wird vornehmlich bei Kücheneinrichtungen, aber auch an Gegenständen des sonstigen Wohnbereichs (Regale, Tische usw.) verarbeitet. Anfangs einfarbig und in der Küche zumeist von weißer Farbe, wird es heute auch „in Dekor" angeboten, außerdem als Holz- und Marmorimitat.)

Als Grundlage für die Analyse der psycho-logischen Gegenständlichkeit des Resopalmöbels sei einleitend eine zusammenfassende Beschreibung der zu ihm explorierten Verhaltens- und Erlebenszusammenhänge gegeben.[1] Sie hält sich möglichst strikt an die Verbalisierung dieser Zusammenhänge durch die Probanden.
Das Resopalmöbel erscheint – wie das Material selbst – vor allem als praktisch, pflegeleicht und solide. Es sei zwar nicht gerade schön, wirke eher kalt, leer, steril und im Vergleich zu Holz irgendwie „tot". Damit könne man sich aber dank seiner vielen praktischen Vorteile leicht abfinden; namentlich sei es sehr bequem sauber zu halten. Verschönernden Maßnahmen entziehe sich das Resopalmöbel aufgrund seiner glatten, unbearbeitbaren Oberfläche völlig; es werde aber schon mal ein Deckchen aufgelegt oder ein Klebebild angebracht. Sachlich und modern, sei das Resopal in der Küche ideal, die müsse schließlich „zack-zack wieder sauber zu machen" und nicht unbedingt gemütlich sein. Sie bekomme zwar durch dieses Material etwas von einem Fabrikations-betrieb oder einem Krankenhaus, aber man halte sich ja in ihr auch nicht länger auf, nur eben zur Erledigung der Kocharbeit. Für die anderen Wohnbereiche sei Holz unbedingt vorzuziehen; das lebe und atme und lasse dem Ausdruck der Persönlichkeit mehr Spielraum. Zwar biete das Resopal auch dort durchaus praktische Lösungen (Arbeitstisch, Regale usw.), würde allerdings Geld keine Rolle spielen, kämen doch eher Holzmöbel in Frage. Sie besäßen mehr Charakter und Stil und in diesem Material seien originellere Lösungen möglich. Holz schmücke auch, und an älteren oder antiken Möbeln habe man zudem etwas von Wert.
In diesem regelmäßig angesprochenen Kontrast zum Holz rücken die funktionalen Aspekte und praktischen Vorteile des Resopals zunehmend in den Hintergrund und wird es dann dominant als unecht, langweilig und „unheimlich gradlinig" charakterisiert; es sei im Grunde abstoßend, da *nur* praktisch. Während zudem Holz wirklich altern könne, und es in langem Gebrauch auch Spuren annehme und damit etwas von seinem Besitzer bzw. eine gemeinsame Geschichte veranschauliche, sei Resopal an-sich zeitlos. Es könne nicht altern, nur unansehnlich werden oder allenfalls kaputtgehen.
Ansonsten ginge alles spurlos an ihm vorüber: Einmal drübergewischt und schon sei es wieder, als wäre nichts gewesen. Während Holz etwas Erzählendes besitze, gebe das Resopal keine Antwort und sei sozusagen erinnerungslos.

13

Weiterhin wird gesagt, dass auf einem Holztisch irgendwelche Flecken, Staub oder Krümel nicht immer unbedingt störend seien, sie könnten in der Maserung untergehen oder mit ihr zusammen irgendwelche Figuren ergeben; dagegen wirkten sie auf Resopal irgendwie aggressiv und ihre sofortige Beseitigung fordernd. Da springe schon das kleinste Bisschen in die Augen, selbst der geringste Fingerabdruck zeichne sich sofort ab, und so müsse man laufend mit dem Lappen hinterher sein, wenn man das Resopal benutzt hat. Natürlich sei auf dem Resopal auch alles leicht zu entfernen, aber es mute einem eben dauernd irgendein Wischen zu; es sei da kompromisslos, und unter diesem Zwang werde man leicht zu seinem Diener.

Diese „Schmutz abweisende" Qualität des Materials und ihre eigentümliche Ambivalenz wurden zum zentralen Thema in den Aussagen der Probanden, wenn sie, auf eine entsprechende Aufforderung hin, ihre Hand für einige Minuten flach auf das Resopal gelegt hatten: Zunächst fühle es sich angenehm kühl und glatt an, vielleicht doch eher ein wenig kalt. Bald aber werde es durch die Körperwärme warm und feucht, schließlich klebrig oder „fischig" kalt und glitschig. Die längere Berührung sei unangenehm bis eklig, wie die eines Toten. Man habe das Gefühl, nicht atmen zu können, nicht genug Körperwärme zu besitzen, um es aufzuwärmen. Das Schwitzen der eigenen Hand werde einem selber widerlich, es wirke „fies" und anormal. Man hinterlasse peinliche feuchte Kränze und erlebe seinen Schweiß als Unsauberkeit, als beschmutzend und kalt. Er sei zwar doch eigentlich etwas Natürliches, aber dennoch fühle man sich von ihm abgestoßen und erfahre sich selbst als abstoßend. Man erlebe eine Ängstlichkeit wie bei einer Prüfung, man klebe fest, es vermische sich, es gebe schließlich keine Trennung mehr zwischen der Sache und einem selbst.

Aus den Phänomenen der Erfahrung und des Umgangs mit dem Resopal, die hier notwendig stark verdichtet wiedergegeben wurden, lassen sich drei Komplexe herausarbeiten, welche die spezifische psycho-logische Gegenständlichkeit dieses Materials kennzeichnen.

Das Resopal wird insgesamt als die perfekte Vergegenständlichung des Ideals makelloser Reinlichkeit realisiert, dessen mühelose Erfüllung es alltäglich möglich mache. Diese stupende Leistung des Resopals, ein extremes Ideal zu setzen und gleichzeitig seine bequeme Erfüllung anzubieten, macht wohl die besondere Faszination dieses Materials aus. In dem, worin es diese immer wieder gepriesene bequeme Erfüllung eines Ideals materialisiert, d. h. in seinen Schmutz abweisenden Eigenschaften, entzieht sich das Resopalmöbel aber zugleich erlebtermaßen jeder Prägung durch seine Benutzung und seinen Benutzer. Und in dieser (durch die Unbearbeitbarkeit seiner Oberfläche noch verstärkten) anschaulichen Erfahrung des Spur(en)losen konstituiert sich das Resopalmöbel psycho-logisch als ein Gegenstand ohne Gesicht und ohne Geschichte. Diese Zeit- und Ausdruckslosigkeit bildet einen ersten Komplex in der psycho-logischen Gegenständlichkeit des Resopalmöbels.

Auf einen zweiten Komplex weisen Aussagen hin wie: den Resopalmöbeln sei nichts Schönes oder Schmückendes eigen und sie entzögen sich auch weitgehend verschönernden Maßnahmen; es bedürfe persönlicher und dekorativer Zugaben, sei dies ein Deckchen, eine alte kupferne Kuchenform o. Ä. (in einem Falle eine Bildtapete mit Waldmotiv), um es mit ihnen aushalten zu können und gemütlich zu haben; diese Möbel seien ausschließlich praktisch und die Beziehungen zu ihnen rein funktionale und allein auf Sauberkeit abgestellt. Auf dem Hintergrund solcher und anderer gleichsinniger Aussagen ist die psycho-logische Gegenständlichkeit des Resopalmöbels als eine eigentümlich dissoziative und partiale zu charakterisieren: In ihr sind tendenziell alle Momente menschlich-gegenständlicher Beziehungen negiert bis auf eines, nämlich das praktisch nützliche; das aber ist ideal gegeben. Dinge von einer solchen, durch ihre Spezialisierung und Perfektionierung bedingten (psycho-logisch) defizitären Gegenständlichkeit sind – um sozusagen auch psychologisch funktionieren zu können – notwendig auf andere, komplementäre Gegenstände angewiesen bzw. erzeugen diese als Nachfrage. Eben jene, welche Baudrillard die „legendären" nannte: das Deckchen, das antike Küchengerät oder ähnliche Dinge mit Gemütswert. (Inzwischen wird auch seitens der Hersteller versucht, dieser psychologisch defizitären Gegenständlichkeit der Resopalmöbel durch Holz- und Marmorimitate beizukommen.)

14

Einen dritten Komplex in der psycho-logischen Gegenständlichkeit der Resopalmöbel bilden die Nötigung zu einem unentwegtem Säubern, die seiner vom Resopal ermöglichten Mühelosigkeit erlebtermaßen entspringt, und die Erfahrung, dass dieses Material bestimmte natürliche, aber nicht funktionale Erscheinungen (Arbeitsspuren, Schweiß usw.) immer gleich als Schmutz denunziert. Von daher wäre die Gegenständlichkeit des Resopalmöbels zu kennzeichnen als eine weniger funktionale denn funktionalisierende. Denn das, was dem Resopalmöbel als materiale Eigenschaft zugesprochen wird, funktional zu sein, konstituiert sich psychologisch darin, dass es das Verhalten seines Benutzers darauf reduziert: Es funktionalisiert ihn, wie es ein Proband ausdrückte, zum „Diener seiner Makellosigkeit".

Wollte man die dem Resopalmöbel eigene (psycho-logische) Gegenständlichkeit insgesamt auf einen knappen Begriff bringen, so könnte man sagen, dass es in seiner psychologischen Realität eigentlich kaum ein Ding darstellt, sondern ein *Funktional*.[2] Und dies nicht etwa nur deshalb, weil es alles das negiert, was ansonsten als die spezifische Gegenständlichkeit eines Möbels ausmachend genannt wird (Gemütlichkeit, Prestige, Stil, Kultiviertheit, Persönlichkeitsausdruck o. Ä.), und es nur noch die eine Qualität besitzt, praktisch zu sein. Sein abstraktes ‚ungegenständliches' Wesen hat weit mehr noch mit jener appellativen Qualität und der eigentümlichen Gewissensfunktion zu tun, die das Resopal in seinem Anspruch auf Makellosigkeit annimmt. Auch ist es wohl eher dieses inquisitorische Moment und nicht die einfache Analogie schweißtreibender Situation, welches die häufigen Prüfungs-Assoziationen erklärt, die bei der längeren Berührung des Materials aufkamen, und was dazu führte, dass der sich sichtbar niederschlagende Schweiß als Makel, als eine sich gegebene Blöße erlebt wurde.

Auf dem Hintergrund der geschilderten psycho-logischen Gegenständlichkeit des Resopalmöbels ist jetzt die spezifische Modellierung zu untersuchen, die es als eine Vergegenständlichung (‚Be-Dingung') sinnlicher Erfahrung eben dieser gibt. Mit anderen Worten, es ist jetzt das Design zu kennzeichnen, das die Sinnlichkeit in den Umgangsqualitäten erhält, die dem Resopalmöbel aufgrund seiner Materialeigenschaften und der daraus resultierenden Form- und Funktionsgestaltung zukommen.

Ausgehend von der Spur(en)losigkeit, in der Benutzung und Benutzer am Resopalmöbel verbleiben, lässt sich als erstes, zentrales Prinzip der von ihm betriebenen Modellierung der Sinnlichkeit eine *Enthistorisierung* der sinnlichen Erfahrung herausstellen. Sowohl in der Bequemlichkeit und Radikalität, die es der Beseitigung von Staub und anderer, seiner Benutzung entspringenden Verunreinigungen eröffnet, als auch in der hohen Resistenz, die es gegen jegliche Abnutzung zeigt, und in seiner Unbearbeitbarkeit, die eine Veränderung gemäß wandelnden Ansprüchen nahezu ausschließt, macht das Resopal Zeit und Geschichtlichkeit tendenziell anschauungslos. Es lässt die Möbel sich sozusagen ihrer Vergangenheit entziehen; man kann zwar *wissen*, dass dieser Resopaltisch schon viele Jahre alt ist, nur *sehen* wird man es nicht, wenn das Resopal hält, was es im Jargon der Kücheneinrichter verspricht: so „zeitlos funktional" und „robust" zu sein, dass es in 10 Jahren noch „brandaktuell" ist.

Mit dieser ‚Zeitlosigkeit' des Resopalmöbels hängt ein anderes Moment in seinem Sinnlichkeitsdesign eng zusammen, das als eine Resultante der vom Resopal betriebenen Enthistorisierung der sinnlichen Erfahrung aufzufassen ist. Dabei geht es um das Erleben der Resopalmöbel als neutral, charakterlos, anonym und abweisend, um die Unmöglichkeit, ihnen (z. B. durch irgendeine Bearbeitung) eine persönliche Note zu geben und sich und seine Geschichte in ihnen wiederzuerkennen. In diesen und anderen, ähnlich um das ‚Gesichtslose' dieser Möbel zentrierten Erfahrungen liegt ein Hinweis darauf, dass in ihrer praktischen und anschaulichen Aneignung ein Anspruch auf individuelle Besonderung unerfüllt bleibt. Dieses an den Resopalmöbeln erlebte Defizit anschaulich-gegenständlicher Selbstwahrnehmung, beziehungsweise die in ihnen auf die Erfahrung der eigenen Funktionalität verkürzte Selbstwahrnehmung, ist als ein Verlust der Anschaulichkeit des Individuellen zu kennzeichnen. Und von daher wäre es zweites Prinzip der dem Resopalmöbel impliziten Modellierung der Sinnlichkeit ein *Depersonalisieren* der sinnlichen Erfahrung herauszustellen.

15

Auf ein anderes Prinzip verweisen die an den Resopalmöbeln gemachten Erfahrungen kompromissloser Funktionalität, die sich in den Aussagen über die ihnen fehlende Gemütlichkeit und ihren technischen Charakter oder in der Einstellung widerspiegelten, dass das Resopal zwar in dem „Arbeitsraum" der Küche durchaus angebracht sei, nicht aber im Wohn- oder Schlafbereich. Darin tritt als ein weiteres Prinzip des im Resopalmöbel gegebenen Sinnlichkeitsdesigns ein *Partialisieren* der sinnlichen Erfahrung zutage. Aus der damit angesprochenen Dissoziation gegenständlicher Beziehungen in solche entweder strikt funktionaler oder aber stimmungs-ästhetischer Natur entstehen dann schließlich zwei grundverschiedene Gattungen des Gegenständlichen. Was namentlich da deutlich wurde, wo durch Deckchen, antikes Küchengerät und andere dekorative Accessoires versucht wurde, der einem Fabrikationsbetrieb ähnlich erlebten Resopal-Küche das hinzuzufügen, was der Erfahrung des Resopalmöbels prinzipiell abgeht: das anschauliche ‚Mehr' des Ästhetischen, ein Moment von ‚Stimmung'. Um dies ein wenig konkreter vor Augen zu haben, vergegenwärtige man sich z. B. die Farbigkeit, die ein Putzen von Möhren auf einem Holztisch ergibt: die verschiedenen Nuancen des Brauns, welche die ihnen etwa noch anhaftende Erde auf dem Holz bildet, die lebendigen Kontraste des Krautgrüns zu den verschiedenen Brauntönen und dem Möhrenrot, die vom Wasser gesetzten Glanzlichter usw. Dann halte man dagegen den scharfen Kontrast, den dies alles zu dem klinischen Weiß eines Resopaltisches bilden würde, und die ‚Abfälligkeit', in die es sogleich alles Abgeschabte und -geschnittene versetzt. Falls die Möhren nicht – wie es dem Resopal-Ambiente eher entsprechen würde – vorgewaschen, vom Kraut befreit und im Plastikbeutel auf den Tisch gekommen sind. Da heißt es dann nur mehr, sie kochfertig würfeln, natürlich auf einem Schneidebrett aus besonders hartem Resopal, damit der Tisch nicht verkratzt wird, und dann beides fix abgewischt und zwischendurch einen beseelenden Blick geworfen auf die an der Wand hängende Reproduktion eines Gemüse-Stilllebens. Ungeachtet der polemischen Nostalgie dieser Illustration, macht sie jene Auflösung der anschaulichen Einheit von Ästhetischem und Praktischem etwas sinnfälliger, die für die vom Resopal vermittelte Beziehung zum Gegenständlichen charakteristisch ist. In dieser Spaltung konstituieren sich schließlich zwei verschiedene, eigenständige Typen von Gegenständlichkeit, eine „legendäre" (Baudrillard) und eine instrumentale; und am Ende dient das einzelne Ding einsinnig entweder dem Vollzug einer Funktion oder der Verrichtung einer Stimmung. Dieses Nebeneinander im Gegenständlichen von Stimmungsdingen und Funktionsdingen stellt die materielle Konsequenz der Partialisierung und Dissoziation sinnlicher Erfahrung dar, die als zentrale Prinzipien des in den Resopalmöbeln angelegten Sinnlichkeitsdesigns hervorgehoben wurden.

Die Darstellung der psycho-logischen Gegenständlichkeit des Resopalmöbels und der in ihm wirksamen Modellierung der sinnlichen Erfahrung ist damit abgeschlossen. Ihre Ergebnisse verdienen einen Kommentar und erlauben zudem einige weitergehende Überlegungen. Aber vorderhand wäre einem möglichen skeptischen Einwand zu begegnen: Wenn das Resopal wirklich die hier beschriebenen prekären psychologischen Implikationen besitzt, wieso findet es dann dennoch so allgemein Verwendung, – was lässt die Probanden trotz ihrer negativen Charakterisierung der Resopalmöbel sich gleichwohl ihrer bedienen? Sie selbst führen zur Erklärung dieses Widerspruchs (auf den sie regelmäßig hingewiesen wurden) immer wieder den „entscheidenden Vorteil" dieser Möbel an, so bequem sauber zu halten zu sein. Die jenem Einwand zugrundeliegende Skepsis hätte also vielmehr der Überwertigkeit zu gelten, die da allgemein dem Ideal der Sauberkeit zukommt, und die es instand setzt, der Rationalisierung selbst solch offener Erfahrungswidersprüche zu dienen.

Allerdings ist auch einzuräumen, dass das Resopal ja beileibe nicht die Perfektion besitzt, die ihm die Werbung nachsagt und von der hier der Prägnanz der Aussagen wegen ausgegangen wurde. Es zeigt ja durchaus, wenn auch nur in geringem Maße, Spuren seiner Benutzung und über die Jahre des Gebrauchs nimmt es schließlich auch gewisse, es vermenschlichende Mucken an. Dass aber vom Resopal dennoch erlebtermaßen eine Störung ausgeht, veranschaulichen die angestrebte Eingrenzung seiner Verwendung auf den häuslichen Arbeitsbereich und die Tendenz, es durch nostalgische Zugaben zu verschönern. Worin unschwer der Versuch zu erkennen ist, die gestörte gegenständliche Selbst-Aneignung selber zu behandeln und der darin widerfahrenen Vereinseitigung entgegenzuwirken.

Die im Umgang mit den Resopalmöbeln wirksame Modellierung der Sinnlichkeit bildet ein Moment dessen, was zwar als ‚materielle Produktion und Reproduktion von Ideologie' viel besprochen ist, aber nur selten auf der Ebene der konkreten Dinge untersucht wird: die gegenständliche, materielle Formierung des Bewusstseins. Mit einer Art Gedankenexperiment ist auf einfache Weise zu demonstrieren, dass die am Resopalmöbel gemachten Erfahrungen mehr als nur unmittelbar praktische und anschauliche sind und mit ihnen nicht nur gegenständliche, sondern auch gesellschaftliche Verhältnisse in die Köpfe kommen (Marx).

Man stelle sich die Situation eines Subjekts vor, in dessen alltäglicher Lebenswelt die genannten Prinzipien der Modellierung des Sinnlichen uneingeschränkt wirksam sind. Unter dem Aspekt einer sinnlichen Erkenntnis der Welt betrachtet, würde in einer derartigen, tendenziell jegliche Anschauung von Geschichte und Individualität entziehenden Umgebung dem Subjekt die Welt gegenübertreten als eine in zeitlos funktionalen Zusammenhängen organisierte. Die alltäglichen gemeinsamen Ordnungen von Ich und Welt erschienen ihm notwendig als ungeschichtliche und in der Objektivität nützlicher Funktionen begründet. Nun stellt ja Geschichte – um hier nur den Aspekt der Enthistorisierung aufzugreifen – psychologisch weder eine Sammlung historischer Daten und Fakten, noch etwa eine Stimmung, sondern den Raum dar, in dem sich Bedeutung organisiert. Wird dieser Raum dem Subjekt unzugänglich, so erscheinen ihm die Bedeutungen notwendig unzeitlich und in sich begründet zu sein. Mit der Kategorie des Geworden-seins tritt aber zugleich die der Veränderbarkeit aus seinem Bewusstsein und spätestens hier erkennt man die Koinzidenz der dem Resopal impliziten Modellierung der Sinnlichkeit und einer ideologischen, den Status quo verabsolutierenden Weltansicht. Als ein gegenständliches Strategem betrachtet[3], betreibt das Resopalmöbel die anschauliche und praktische Selbstverständlichung einer ahistorischen und rein funktionalen Beziehung zur Welt. Es leistet eine ganz alltägliche, aber darum nur um so plausiblere Objektivation einer aufs Hier-und-Jetzt fixierten, von Individuellem abstrahierenden, am ‚wertfrei' Funktionalen und auf Effizienz ausgerichteten Mentalität[4].

So gesehen stellt also z. B. eine perfekte Resopal-Küche, deren psychologischer Aufriss hier unter den Begriffen Enthistorisierung, Depersonalisation, Funktionalisierung (usw.) nachgezeichnet wurde, ein hoch ideologisches Ambiente dar. Sie funktioniert sozusagen als häusliche Vorschule einer Mentalität, deren kulturelle und politische Konsequenzen sich zwar inzwischen in jedem höheren Feuilleton beklagt finden, aber die im Zusammenhang ihrer alltäglichen gegenständlichen Vermittlung zu untersuchen, man sich geflissentlich erspart. Nämliches trifft auch auf die ‚Materialistische Persönlichkeitstheorie' zu, der doch eine Analyse der materiellen (Re-)Produktion von Ideologie angelegentlich sein müsste. Sie hält es aber, wohl aus Gründen wissenschaftlicher Reputation, eher mit dem traditionellen Filigran von Interaktion und Sozialisation, statt einmal zu untersuchen, wie sich die Verhältnisse ‚aufmöbeln', um so – gewissermaßen gegenständlich konnotiert – über alltägliche Gewohnheitsbildungen schließlich in die Köpfe zu kommen.

Um die etwas allgemein gewordenen Überlegungen zum Abschluss noch einmal an Konkretem aufzugreifen, eine Bemerkung zu dem jugendlichen „Vandalismus", über den die Pädagogen heute so bewegt Klage führen und dessen Auftreten gerade in modernen, neu errichteten Schulen ihnen so publikumswirksames Kopfzerbrechen bereitet[5].

Wirklich, der Besuch eines solchen Schulbaus, namentlich einer Ganztagsschule, kann einige Verwirrung stiften: Welch ein Kontrast nicht selten zwischen dieser modernen, kinderfreundlich robusten, nachgerade fröhlich unverwüstlichen Einrichtung (alles abwaschbar, kratzfest usw.) und der überall herrschenden Unordnung, der oft fast schon methodisch wirkenden Verschmutzung. – Und doch kein Widerspruch, wie sich einem bald eröffnet. Denn in einem Environment derart panischer Solidität, in dem alles sofort und garantiert spurenlos wieder in Ordnung zu bringen ist – wie soll sich da einer bemerkbar machen, sich seiner selbst, seines Einwohnens oder seines Widerstandes anschaulich vergewissern können anders, als mit Unordnung und groben Schikanen? Dass diese so ‚vandalistische' Züge annehmen, ist angesichts der demonstrativen – ebenso permissiv gemeinten wie provozierend wirkenden – Unverwüstlichkeit der Einrichtung nachgerade zwangsläufig. Das liegt eher in der Natur der Sache als am Charakter der Subjekte.

17

Man vergegenwärtige sich dagegen die Schule, die man selber vor Jahrzehnten besucht hat, wo in den Graffiti der Bänke und Wände die Geschichte der Großen Renitenz für die Nachkommenden überliefert und fortzuführen war; wo sich am Mobiliar die geschlagenen Schlachten bezeugt fanden und man an der Decke, in den Schwammabdrücken und den dort klebenden Löschpapierkugeln, sich seiner von Langeweile getriebenen Kühnheiten immer wieder vergewissern konnte (usw.). Dann wird man auf dem Hintergrund der hier am Resopalmöbel exemplarisch aufgezeigten Verhältnisse gegenständlicher Selbst-Aneignung die Erklärung jenes „Vandalismus" nicht in dem narzisstisch Objekt verneinenden Charakter eines „neuen Sozialisationstypus" (Ziehe)[6] suchen müssen. Man hätte sich vielmehr der verneinten Gegenständlichkeit zuzuwenden und sie auf ihre psychologischen Implikationen hin zu untersuchen. Dabei würde dann diese Attacke gegen die Dinge sehr bald verständlich als die Notwehr eines Subjekts gegen eine Gegenständlichkeit, in der sein Anspruch auf anschauliche Selbst-Aneignung so gründlich negiert wird, dass er nur mehr in ihrer Demolierung erfüllbar ist. Als Fazit aus dieser Studie zum Resopalmöbel ist festzuhaken, dass in der dem Psychischen durch die Dinge gegebenen Modellierung nicht etwa nur die sinnliche Erfahrung spezifisch formiert wird, nicht allein ‚Perzepte' vermittelt, sondern dem Subjekt übergreifende Konzepte von sich und seiner Welt eingetragen werden. Als deren Materialisation bilden die Dinge – psychologisch betrachtet – gegenständliche Strageme einer Weltanschauung, sind sie in der am Resopalmöbel aufgezeigten Weise ‚Konkrete Ideologie'.

1: Die Studie stützt sich auf psychologische Explorationen zu diesem Thema, die im Jahre 1977 unter meiner Leitung von Dr. phil. Wolfgang Baßler (Dipl.-Psych.) und von Dipl.-Psych. Regina Strahlka im Rahmen eines Praktikums am Psychologischen Institut II (Lehrstuhl l) der Universität zu Köln durchgeführt wurden.
2: In der abstrakten, eigentlich nur als ‚Resistenz' fassbaren Materialität des Resopals und in der schieren Funktionalität, die das Resopalmöbel auszeichnen, wird dieses zu einem eigentümlich ungegenständlichen Ding und belegt es gewissermaßen die psycho-logische Existenz von ‚Undingen'. Vgl. dazu das Kapitel über das „Plastik", in: Roland Barthes: Mythen des Alltags, Frankfurt a. M. 1970, S. 79ff.
3: Dazu, dass im Gebrauch der Dinge mehr als nur ihre praktische Funktion realisiert und immer auch eine allgemeine ‚Botschaft' angeeignet wird, vgl. auch Roland Barthes: Elemente der Semiologie, Frankfurt a. M. 1979, S. 35f. Er spricht da von einer „universellen Semantisierung des Gebrauchs", die er damit zusammenbringt, dass, „da unsere Gesellschaft nur standardisierte, normalisierte Gegenstände erzeugt, diese Gegenstände zwangsläufig die Realisierung eines Modells, die Worte einer Sprache, die Substanz einer signifikanten Form sind", a.a.O., S. 36.
4: Vgl. dazu Baudrillards Kritik an dem funktionalistischen Diktat, dem seines Erachtens nach die Dinge heute allgemein unterworfen seien; Jean Baudrillard: Das System der Dinge. Über unser Verhältnis zu den alltäglichen Gegenständen, Frankfurt a. M. 2007, S. 76ff.
5: Vgl. Helga Häsing, Herbert Stubenrauch, Thomas Ziehe (Hg.): Narziß – ein neuer Sozialisationstypus, Bensheim 1980.
6: Vgl. ebd. und Thomas Ziehe: Pubertät und Narzißmus. Sind Jugendliche entpolitisiert?, Frankfurt a. M./Köln 1975.

Zuerst erschienen in: Friedrich Wolfram Heubach: Das bedingte Leben. Theorie der psycho-logischen Gegenständlichkeit der Dinge. Ein Beitrag zur Psychologie des Alltags, München 1987. Wiederabdruck in geänderter Fassung mit freundlicher Genehmigung des Autors.

FORMICA FURNITURE, OR THE SENSES DON'T JUST TAKE THINGS IN – THEY TAKE ON A FORM WITHIN THEM: EVERY DESIGN OF OBJECTS IS ALSO A DESIGN OF SENSORY EXPERIENCE

(The plastic sold under the brand name "Formica" and used for coating surfaces is employed primarily in kitchens but also for objects in other parts of the house (shelves, tables, etc.). Initially monochromatic (and in kitchens predominantly white), today it is also offered in "decorator" colors and finishes, including imitation wood and marble.)

As the basis for my analysis of the psycho-logical object character of Formica furniture, I begin with a summary of the experiences and behaviors associated with it by the subjects of our study.[1] My description hews as closely as possible to the verbalization of those phenomena by the participants.
Like Formica itself, Formica furniture is above all seen as practical, low-maintenance, and sturdy. Although it isn't attractive but seems cold, empty, sterile, and somehow "dead" in comparison with wood, these are things

one can easily learn to live with thanks to its many practical advantages, especially the fact that it is extremely easy to keep clean. Formica furniture completely defies all attempts to beautify it due to its smooth, unworkable surface; one can, however, place a small cloth on top of it or a sticker. Functional and modern, Formica is perfect for the kitchen, which one has to be able to clean "in two seconds" and which doesn't necessarily have to be comfortable. True, a Formica kitchen bears a certain resemblance to a factory or a hospital, but one doesn't spend long hours there in any case, only as long as it takes to do the cooking. For other parts of the house, wood is definitely preferable; it lives and breathes and leaves more room for expressing one's personality. Although Formica offers practical solutions there too (work table, shelves, etc.), if money were no object one would gravitate toward wooden furniture. It has more character and style, and as a material wood allows for more creative solutions. Moreover, wood is decorative, and with old or antique furniture one has something of value.

When the subject turns to the contrast with wood, as it regularly does, Formica's functional aspects and practical advantages increasingly recede into the background and Formica is then primarily described as boring, artificial, and "incredibly no-nonsense"; at bottom it is repulsive, because it is exclusively practical. Moreover, while wood can genuinely age and takes on traces over long years of use, providing tangible, visual evidence of its owner or a common history, Formica is timeless. It cannot age but can only become unsightly or at most break.

Otherwise, everything passes over it without a trace; a single wipe and it's as if nothing had happened. While wood seems to tell a story, Formica, as it were, doesn't answer; it has no memory.

The study participants also said that on a wooden table stains, dust, or crumbs are not necessarily a problem, since they can be absorbed into the grain or combine with it to form patterns. On Formica, however, they somehow appear aggressive and seem to insist on being immediately removed. Even the smallest quantity of them stands out; even the slightest fingerprint is immediately visible, so one always has to wipe Formica off as soon as one is finished using it. Of course, on Formica everything is easy to remove, but it constantly insists on being wiped off for one reason or another; in this respect it is uncompromising, and under this pressure one can easily become its servant.

This "dirt-repellent" quality of Formica and its peculiar ambivalence became a central theme in the volunteers' statements when asked to lay their hand flat on the material for several minutes at a time. At first, it felt pleasantly cool and smooth, if perhaps a little cold. Soon, however, their body heat made it warm and damp, eventually turning it sticky or else "clammy," cold, and slippery. Prolonged contact with Formica was at the very least experienced as unpleasant, with some participants describing it as disgusting, like touching a dead body. Subjects reported feeling as if they couldn't breathe, as if they didn't have enough body heat to warm it up. They began to find the sweat of their own palms disgusting; it seemed "nasty" and abnormal. One leaves embarrassing damp marks, the participants said, and experiences one's sweat as something unclean, as something sullying and cold. Although it is actually something natural, one nevertheless feels repulsed by it and experiences oneself as repulsive. One feels the kind of anxiety associated with taking a test; one sticks; one seems to physically mingle with the Formica; there ultimately ceases to be any distinction between the material and oneself.

Based on these descriptions of the experiences and behaviors associated with Formica, which have necessarily been reported here in highly compressed form, three complexes may be identified that characterize the specific psycho-logical object character of this material.

Overall, Formica is regarded as the perfect objectification of the ideal of spotless cleanness, whose effortless fulfillment it makes an everyday occurrence. It is probably this tremendous achievement, the fact that Formica proposes an extreme ideal while also making it easy to fulfill, that constitutes its special fascination. And yet in the manner in which it materializes this consistently touted easy realization of an ideal – that is, in its dirt-repellent properties – Formica furniture is also experienced as rejecting any imprint of its user or use. And in this concrete, visual experience of the total absence of traces (which is further reinforced by the unworkability of its surface), Formica furniture is psycho-logically constituted as an object with no face and no history. This atemporality and expressionlessness represents the first complex within the psychological object character of Formica furniture.

A second complex is suggested by statements like these: there is nothing beautiful or decorative about Formica furniture, and it largely defies all beautifying measures; it takes personal and decorative additions to be able to live with and feel at home with it, be it a small cloth, an old copper cake pan, or something similar (in one case wallpaper with a forest theme); Formica furniture is exclusively practical, and one's relations with it are purely functional and geared exclusively toward cleanliness. In light of these and similar statements, the psycho-logical object character of Formica furniture emerges as peculiarly dissociative and partial. In it, all aspects of the relationship between human beings and objects are negated except for one, that of practical utility; however, that single aspect is ideally fulfilled. Things like this, which are so specialized and perfect that their object character is (psycho-logically) deficient, are necessarily dependent – in order, so to speak, to be able to function psychologically as well – on other, complementary objects or else create a demand for such objects. Precisely those which Baudrillard terms "mythical": doilies, antique kitchen utensils, and similar things with emotional value. (Manufacturers have now begun to attempt to mitigate the psychologically deficient object character of Formica furniture by offering it in imitation wood and marble.)

A third complex within the psycho-logical object character of Formica furniture comes to light in the experience that because Formica is so easy to clean one is constantly forced to clean it, and in the perception that this material always immediately shows up certain natural but nonfunctional phenomena (traces of work, sweat, etc.) as dirt. In this sense, Formica furniture's object character is actually not so much functional as functionalizing. For what is ascribed to Formica furniture as a material property – its functional quality – has its psychological manifestation in the reduction of the user's behavior to this aspect alone: it functionalizes the user, turning him or her, as one subject put it, into a "servant of its spotlessness."
If we wished to sum up the peculiar (psycho-logical) object character of Formica furniture in a single term, we might say that in its psychological reality it is not so much a thing as it is a *function*.[2] And not just because it negates everything else that is seen as constituting the specific object character of a piece of furniture (comfort, prestige, style, refinement, personal expression, etc.), because it only possesses a single quality: practicality. Its abstract, "un-object-like" character has far more to do with the "hortatory" quality and peculiar conscience-like function developed by Formica in its insistence on spotlessness. Indeed, it is no doubt this inquisitorial moment rather than the simple analogy with other sweat-inducing situations that explains the frequent associations with examinations and tests that came up on prolonged contact with it and that led the participants to experience the visible accumulation of sweat as a blemish or taint, as something mildly shameful or humiliating.

Against the backdrop of the psycho-logical object character of Formica furniture depicted above, I now consider the specific ways in which such furniture, as a conditioning and objectification of sensory experience, molds that experience. In other words, I now attempt to characterize the design acquired by the sensible in the type of interaction that Formica furniture encourages through its material properties and resulting formal and functional characteristics.
Taking as our starting point the experience that neither user nor use leave any trace on Formica furniture, we may identify the *dehistoricization* of sensory experience as the first and most fundamental principle of its molding of the sensible. In the convenience and radicality it gives to the elimination of dust and other impurities resulting from its use, in its high degree of resistance to wear and tear of any kind, and in its unworkability,

which makes it virtually impossible to alter it in accord with changing demands, Formica in principle deprives time and historicity of any visual manifestation. It causes the furniture, as it were, to escape its past. While one may *know* that a certain Formica table is many years old, one will not be able to *see* it so long as Formica keeps the promise it makes in the jargon of the kitchen designers: to be so "timelessly functional" and "rugged" that in ten years it will still be "brand new."

This "timelessness" of Formica furniture is closely related to another aspect of its design of the sensible, a dimension that may be seen as a result of Formica's dehistoricization of sensory experience. I am referring to the experience of Formica furniture as neutral, lacking character, anonymous, and off-putting, to the impossibility of lending it a personal note (e.g. by working it in some way) or of recognizing oneself and one's history in it. These and other experiences of the "faceless" quality of this furniture suggest that in its practical and visual acquisition a demand for individuation goes unfulfilled. This experience of Formica furniture as failing to provide one with a visual and objective perception of oneself, or as reducing that self-perception to the experience of one's functionality, may be described as the loss of any visual manifestation of individuality. We may therefore identify the second principle of Formica furniture's implicit molding of the sensible as a *depersonalization* of sensory experience.

Another principle is suggested by the experiences of Formica furniture's uncompromising functionality reflected in the statements concerning its technical character or its lack of comfort or "hominess," and in the view that Formica is entirely appropriate in the "work space" of the kitchen but not in the living room or bedroom. These experiences suggest that another principle of Formica furniture's design of the sensible is a *partialization* of sensory experience. The dissociation of relations with objects into those which are strictly functional and those which are purely atmospheric and aesthetic ultimately results in the creation of two fundamentally different types of objects. This surfaced quite clearly where doilies, antique kitchen utensils, and other decorative accessories were used in an attempt to add what is fundamentally missing from the experience of Formica furniture to the Formica kitchen with its air of a manufacturing plant: the visible "surplus" of the aesthetic, a moment of "atmosphere" or "mood." In order to visualize this a little bit more concretely, imagine the colorful display created by the act of washing carrots on a wooden table: the various shades of brown produced on the wood by any dirt that may still be clinging to them, the vivid contrast between the green carrot tops and the various browns and the orange of the carrots, the glinting of the water, etc. Now consider the stark contrast that all of this would form to the clinical whiteness of a Formica table, and how the latter would immediately set off the cuttings and peelings as garbage. Unless of course the carrots – as would be much more in keeping with the ambience of Formica – were to arrive on the table in a plastic bag, prewashed and with their tops removed. In which case all that remains to do is to chop them up, naturally on a cutting board of especially hard Formica so as not to scratch the table, and then quickly wipe off both table top and cutting board while now and then casting an inspiring glance at the reproduction of a vegetable still life hanging on the wall. Despite the polemical nostalgia of this example, it makes the dissolving of the visible unity of the aesthetic and the practical which is characteristic of the relationship to the object world communicated by Formica somewhat clearer. This division ultimately leads to the creation of two distinct and independent types of objects, the "mythical" (Baudrillard) and the instrumental. In the end, a particular object does one of two things: it either performs a function or creates a mood, but not both. This juxtaposition in the object world of atmospheric and functional things is the material consequence of the partialization and dissociation of sensory experience that I have highlighted as central principles of Formica furniture's implicit design of the sensible.

This completes my presentation of the psycho-logical object character of Formica furniture and its molding of sensory experience. My conclusions call for some commentary as well as suggesting certain additional reflections. First, however, I would like to respond to a possible skeptical objection: if Formica really has the precarious psychological implications I have described, then why is it nevertheless so widely used? Why is it that despite their negative characterizations of Formica, the subjects still continue to use it? In explaining this contradiction (which was regularly pointed out to them), they themselves consistently cite the "decisive advantage" of Formica furniture, the fact that it is so easy to keep clean. Thus, the skepticism underlying that objection should really be directed against the excessive importance generally ascribed to the ideal of cleanness, which enables it to rationalize even blatant experiential contradictions like this one.

At the same time, it must be admitted that Formica by no means possesses the perfection claimed by its advertisers, but which I have nonetheless taken as the basis for this essay because of the pointedness of the statements. It does show traces of use, albeit only to a limited extent, and over long use it ultimately acquires certain humanizing idiosyncrasies. That there is nonetheless something disturbing about it is illustrated by the effort to limit its use to the work areas of the household and the tendency to beautify it with nostalgic additions. Both of these are clear attempts to remedy the disturbed mechanism of object-based self-acquisition oneself and to counteract the one-sidedness encountered there.

The molding of the sensible that operates in the interaction with Formica furniture is one aspect of a subject that, while much discussed as the "material production and reproduction of ideology," is rarely studied at the level of concrete things: the object-based, material formation of consciousness. It is easy to show through a kind of thought experiment that these experiences of Formica furniture are more than purely practical and visual ones and that the conditions they impress on our minds are not just objective but also social (Marx).

Imagine a subject in whose everyday life the above-mentioned principles of the molding of the sensible reign unchecked. Considered from the perspective of a sensory knowledge of the world, an environment of this kind, which in principle defies any visible manifestation of history or individuality, would make it seem to the subject that the world is organized into timeless functional relationships. The everyday shared systems of self and world would necessarily appear to such a subject as ahistorical and grounded in the objectivity of useful functions. Now psychologically, history – to restrict ourselves here to the aspect of dehistoricization – is neither a collection of facts and figures nor an atmosphere or mood but the space in which meaning is organized.

If this space becomes inaccessible to the subject, meanings will necessarily seem to it to be atemporal and self-existing. With the category of historical becoming, however, that of alterability also disappears from its consciousness, and here it becomes apparent, if it hasn't already, that there is a coincidence between Formica's implicit molding of the sensible and an ideological world view that absolutizes the status quo. Regarded as an object-based stratagem,[3] Formica furniture brings about the visible and practical naturalization of an ahistorical and purely functional relationship to the world. It realizes the utterly mundane but hence all the more plausible objectification of a mentality fixated on the here and now, which abstracts from individuality and is oriented toward "value-neutral" functionality and efficiency.[4]

Seen in this way, then, a perfect Formica kitchen, whose "psychological floor plan" I have sketched here through the concepts of dehistoricization, depersonalization, functionalization, etc., is actually a highly ideological environment. It functions, as it were, as a kind of domestic preschool for a mentality whose cultural and political consequences are now lamented in all the more sophisticated arts and culture sections and yet whose examination in the context of its everyday object-based transmission is carefully avoided. The same is true of "materialist personality theory," which might be expected to regard the material (re)production of ideology as a matter of pressing concern. However, no doubt for reasons of academic reputation, it primarily keeps to the traditional filigree of interaction and socialization, instead of for once investigating how general conditions turn into concrete habitats – as it were with objective connotations – in order to ultimately enter our minds through everyday habit formations.

To conclude with a concrete application of these observations, which have taken a somewhat general turn, I now consider the subject of youthful "vandalism," which teachers today complain about so bitterly and whose occurrence precisely in newly built modern schools has them tearing their hair out to such powerful public effect.[5]

It really can be somewhat bewildering to visit one of these school buildings, especially one that houses an all-day school. The contrast is often quite stark between the modern, child-friendly, rugged, almost cheerfully indestructible facility (where everything is washable, scratchproof, etc.) and the universal chaos that reigns there, a sullying that often seems almost methodical. And yet it is no contradiction, as soon becomes apparent. For in an environment of such terrifying ruggedness, where everything can be cleaned up immediately and is guaranteed to leave no trace, how is one to make one's presence felt, how can one visibly affirm oneself, one's inhabiting of the space, or one's resistance except by creating chaos and playing crude pranks? Given the institution's ostentatious indestructibility – which is as provocative in its effects as it is permissive in its intentions – it is almost inevitable that these pranks should become acts of "vandalism." This has more to do with the situation itself than it does with the character of the subjects.

Now imagine the school you attended decades ago, where in the graffiti that covered the benches and walls the History of the Great Unruliness was handed down for later generations to consume and continue; where the battles fought were documented by the furniture; and where one could always affirm one's boredom-driven exploits by looking at the ceiling, at the sponge marks and the spitballs still sticking there, etc. Do this, and in light of the conditions of object-based self-acquisition developed here through the example of Formica furniture, you will no longer have to go looking for the explanation of this "vandalism" in the narcissistic, object-negating character of a "new type of socialization" (Ziehe).[6] Instead, one should turn to the negated objective environment itself and examine it in terms of its psychological implications. Then this assault on things would very quickly become comprehensible as the subject's self-defense against an objective environment in which its right to visible self-acquisition is so thoroughly negated that it can only be fulfilled by demolishing that environment.

Ultimately, the lesson of this investigation of Formica furniture is that in the molding of psychology by things it is not just sensory experience that is specifically formed, not just "percepts" that are transmitted; rather, the subject is inculcated with overarching concepts of itself and its world. From a psychological perspective, things – as the material embodiment of these concepts – are object-based stratagems of a world view; they are, as I have sought to make clear through the example of Formica furniture, "concrete ideology."

1: This essay is based on psychological explorations of this subject conducted under my supervision in 1977 by Dr. phil. Wolfgang Baßler (Dipl.-Psych.) and Dipl.-Psych. Regina Strahlka during a practical traineeship at the Institute of Psychology II (Department I) of the University of Cologne.

2: In Formica's abstract materiality, which in fact can only be grasped as "resistance," and in the sheer functionality that distinguishes Formica furniture, the latter becomes a strangely "un-object-like" thing which effectively demonstrates the psycho-logical existence of "Undinge" [literally "un-things," a German word whose dictionary meaning is "absurdities" – The translator]. See the chapter on "Plastic", in: Roland Barthes, *Mythologies: The Complete Edition, In a New Translation*, trans. Richard Howard and Annette Lavers (New York, 2012), pp. 193–95.

3: For more on the notion that when things are used, more is realized than their practical function alone, and that a general "message" is always received as well, see Roland Barthes, *Elements of Semiology*, trans. Annette Lavers and Colin Smith (New York, 1968). Barthes speaks there of a "universal semantization of usages," which he relates to the fact that, "since our society produces only standardized, normalized objects, these objects are unavoidably realizations of a model, the speech of a language, the substances of significant form" (pp. 41–42).

4: See Baudrillard's critique of the functionalist tyranny, to which in his view objects are universally subject today; Jean Baudrillard, *The System of Objects*, trans. James Benedict (New York, 1996), pp. 57ff.

5: See Helga Häsing, Herbert Stubenrauch, and Thomas Ziehe, eds., *Narziß – ein neuer Sozialisationstypus* (Bensheim, 1980).

6: See ibid. as well as Thomas Ziehe, *Pubertät und Narzißmus. Sind Jugendliche entpolitisiert?* (Frankfurt a. M./Cologne, 1975).

First published in Friedrich Wolfram Heubach, *Das bedingte Leben. Theorie der psycho-logischen Gegenständlichkeit der Dinge. Ein Beitrag zur Psychologie des Alltags* (Munich, 1987). Reprinted here in modified form with the generous permission of the author.

WEBEN

„At this point in time, artists who happen to be women need this particular form of hysteria like they need a hole in the head." – Bridget Riley, 1972

Penelope

Es gibt unterschiedliche Gründe, um sich der Tätigkeit des Webens zu widmen. Penelope webte, um viele Jahre der Erwartung zu überstehen. Während ihr Mann Odysseus bekanntlich die Welt erkundete, wurde sie von zahlreichen Freiern bedrängt, die sie sich nur dank einer List vom Leibe halten konnte. Denn ihre Verfügbarkeit machte sie vom Abschluss ihrer Webarbeit abhängig, wobei sie nachts aufdröselte, was sie tagsüber geschaffen hatte. Es braucht viele Fäden, bis ein feines Tuch entsteht, mit ihnen eingewoben sind Zeit, Energie, Geschichte. Alexandra Bircken beschäftigt sich oft mit der Frage, wie sich das eine mit dem anderen verbinden lässt, und wie doch alles mit allem zusammenhängt. Das Spektrum der Materialien ist umfassend: natürliche Dinge, Überbleibsel verlassener Vogelnester, Äste, Haare oder Wachs, Materialien wie Wolle, Stoffe, Gummi, ebenso Plastik, Metall sowie gefundene und wieder verwertbare Objekte kommen gleichermaßen zum Zug. Nur eines ist ihrer heterogenen Dingwelt gemein: Die Objekte sind unhandlich, widerspenstig, schwer formbar und ursprünglich nicht als Elemente für Skulpturen bestimmt. Bircken webt die als nutzlos angeschwemmten Dinge in installative Trag- und Spannstrukturen ein und kommt auf diese Weise zu eigenwilligen, heterogenen Gebilden, die zwitterhaft im Raum existieren, als abstrakte Form und Verweissystem gelebter Populärkultur zugleich.

Mrs. Willard

Weben gehört klassischerweise der symbolischen Ordnung des Weiblichen an. Auch Mrs. Willard, eine Figur in Sylvia Plaths Roman *Glasglocke,* verschreibt sich der Tätigkeit des Webens.[1] Allerdings steht das Weben hier eher für die Vergeblichkeit als für eine mögliche Rettung. Regelmäßig stellt Mrs. Willard aus den alten Anzügen ihres Mannes Webteppiche her, nur, um diese nach mühevoller Arbeit als Fußmatten zu nutzen und dem sofortigen Verschleiß preiszugeben. Ähnlich wie Mrs. Willard nutzt auch Bircken oft gebrauchte Textilien für ihre gewebten Plastiken, allerdings verkehrt sie Aspekte wie Zerrissenheit und Vergeblichkeit in Selbstbewusstsein und Feierlichkeit. Ihr künstlerisches Vorgehen folgt demjenigen von Louise Bourgeois, die es wie folgt beschrieb: „Ich mache etwas, ich zerstöre es, ich mache es neu und ich komme immer wieder darauf zurück. Es ist ein Privileg zu sublimieren. Viele Leute können nicht sublimieren. Sie haben keinen Zugang zu ihrem Unbewussten."[2]

24

Birckens Ausstellungen heißen *Blondie* oder *Hausrat,* ihre Werke kommen als *Twiggy* (2012) daher oder fordern bei *Uknit Bonn* (2012) im Wortspiel gleichermaßen zum Stricken und zum Zusammenschluss[3] auf. Auch hier ist von List zu sprechen, wenn Bircken diese so durch und durch mit stereotypen Konnotationen besetzten Bereiche für sich reklamiert und die klassisch tradierten Zeichen noch einmal in aller Deutlichkeit inszeniert. Haben wir es nicht schon so oft gehört? Wir wissen es: Frauen stricken und weben und sollen sich verbünden, sie lieben weiche Materialien und Handgemachtes, sind bedacht auf Bezüge und Beziehungen, und sie sind neuerdings dank des Zuspruchs einer hohen sozialen Kompetenz auf dem Arbeitsmarkt doch noch gefragt. Bircken belebt diese klassischen Vorstellungen, indem sie sie konsequent wieder aufführt, sie theatralisch im Raum installiert und die Betrachter Zeugen einer heiteren und zugleich dramatischen Inszenierung werden lässt. Wir verstricken uns in Geweben und Netzen, in ihrer Dichte und in ihrer Doppelbödigkeit, bis wir uns sicher sind, dass der Professor oder Bankdirektor eine „Blondie" ist, dass die mächtige Schaltzentrale, Ort der Wissens- und Geldproduktion, von Hausrat umgeben ist, dass der Anzugträger eine „Twiggy" darstellt und anstelle von Smartphones das Stricken angesagt ist.

Christoph Kolumbus

Nicht nur das Weben, das Textile schlechthin wird der Domäne der Frau zugesprochen. Nicht wenige Künstlerinnen sind uns entsprechend bekannt, die dem formlosen, den Körper mehr oder weniger verhüllenden und schützenden Material zugewandt sind. Lange Zeit gehörte es in der Geschichte der Kunst zur meisterlichen (männlichen) Aufgabenstellung, den textilen Faltenwurf aus den Niederungen des Handwerklichen in die hohe Kunst auf Leinwand oder in Marmor zu übertragen. Das Material Stoff, das für sich keine Form besitzt, sondern sich anpasst und anschmiegt, hält erst seit den späten 60er Jahren, mit künstlerischen Tendenzen des Post-Minimalismus wie „Eccentric Abstraction" oder „Anti-Form", Einzug in das Materialieninventar der Kunst. Bekanntlich waren es besonders Künstlerinnen, die zu diesen neuen Formen der Skulptur entscheidend beigetragen haben. Dabei bleibt erstaunlich, dass das Textile und das Weben so lange als minderwertig angesehen wurden, zieht man den großen Einfluss dieser Kulturleistung in Betracht, die bis in die heutige digitale und globale Welt reicht. Seth Siegelaub, Theoretiker der Konzeptkunst und Erforscher der Geschichte des Webens, bringt die Tatsache, dass Christoph Kolumbus aus einem Haus der Weber stammte, zugespitzt mit weit reichenden Errungenschaften der Menschheit in Verbindung: „The intimate relationship between textiles and society can also be seen in the fundamental role it played in the rise of the capitalist system, as the first large-scale capitalist industry (the production and export of wool in medieval Flanders); in the industrial revolution (the mechanization of cotton spinning and weaving in eighteenth-century England); in architecture, as the object of the first multi-storied iron frame building (Bage's flax mill in Shrewsbury, England in 1796); as the subject of the first working-class history (Henson's history of the framework-knitters in 1831); or as the subject of the first semiotic text (Roland Barthes, La Mode, Paris 1963); not to mention that the French word for loom is the same as the general word for profession or trade (‚métier'), and the German word for textiles is the same as the general word for material or matter (‚Stoffe'), which is also the case for the Dutch word ‚stof', as well as in English, with the word ‚material'. [...] Perhaps it is by chance that Christopher Columbus, like his father, was first a wool weaver and wool merchant, but it is quite logical that the Jacquard loom in early nineteenth-century France was the inspiration for the work of Charles Babbage in England which lead directly to the invention of the computer in the twentieth century."[4]

Die Struktur des Textilen, die kulturhistorisch für viele Entwicklungen in anderen Lebensbereichen so folgenreich ist, interessiert auch Bircken. Jeder Stoff und jedes Gewebe besteht aus einer Vielzahl einzelner, miteinander verschränkter Elemente, die nur in ihrer Summe (wieder ist die Gemeinschaft angesprochen!) erfolgreich sein können. Hinzu kommt, dass es sich stets um bewegliche, dehnbare, mehr oder weniger flexible und veränderliche Gewebe handelt: Nylonstrümpfe mit Spitzen und Spickeln spannen sich patchworkartig vernäht zu Wandbekleidungen auf und mutieren zu Tierfellen, bekannt als Jagdtrophäen und Platzhalter viriler

Potenz (*Skin 2,* 2010). Birckens Nylonstrümpfe bleiben weiterhin verführerisch – so ihre Bestimmung als Strumpf wie auch als Kunstwerk – und erscheinen zugleich als Haut eines gefährlichen Tiers, wie es von Kolumbus in der neuen Welt hätte vorgefunden werden können. In logischer Konsequenz finden sich auch andere „Überreste" von Erlegtem: *Knochen* (2011) oder aber skalpähnliche Gebilde (*Pamela Combat,* 2010, gemeinsames Werk mit Thomas Brinkmann). Selbstverständlich sucht Bircken auf ihrem künstlerischen Weg ebenso wie Kolumbus (oder Adam) die exotischen oder verbotenen Früchte mit libidinösem Inneren (*Bundle,* 2007, *Was soll das,* 2008) und lässt sich auch von gespenstischen Dämonen nicht abschrecken (*Tentakel,* 2009).

Kleider für Räume, Räume an- und ausziehen
Bircken, die ursprünglich Modedesign studierte und deren Werk sich als eine Herauslösung aus diesem Feld begreifen lässt, schafft Kleider für Räume, ohne jemals zu vergessen, dass Kleider Leute machen. „Clothing, more than any other object or possession, is closely identified with the body of the absent wearer."[5] Gefundene Textilien und von der Künstlerin selbst dazu gestrickte und gestickte Partien formen *Bündel* (2009), eine Bodenskulptur, die einem Sitzschemel ähnlich im Raum steht. An einzelnen Stellen lassen sich Pullover oder T-Shirts, die ihrer Funktion enthoben sind, erkennen. Sie sind als Chiffren des Heute lesbar, mögen auch an Bilder menschlicher Not erinnern und bleiben zugleich abstrakte Form, Sockel und Skulptur zugleich. Die starke Bindung, die zwischen Kleidung und Träger besteht, nutzt Bircken, wenn sie mit textilen Strukturen den Raum auskleidet: Gewobenes schiebt sich wortwörtlich als abstraktes Muster in einem Spannsystem in die Architektur ein (*Insert,* 2009) oder bietet sich als Fläche dar, die das Geschehen im Raum aufnehmen will (*Receptor,* 2009). Bei *Uknit Bonn* (2012) wiederum nutzt Bircken Metall, um Maschen zu suggerieren, die einen Raum auf ganzer Länge auskleiden. Der Verweis auf martialische Ritterrüstungen verkehrt sich in Handgestricktes, das mit einer Reihe Maschen, die tatsächlich aus der Reihe tanzen, ausgestattet ist.[6] Auch hier sind Gleichzeitigkeiten bei der Lesart eingeschrieben, denn neben den kultur- und sozialpolitischen Implikationen sind immer auch formalästhetische Gesichtspunkte angesprochen. Das metallene Kleid wirft das einfallende Licht im Raum zurück und trägt so – wenn die Maschenfläche zu flimmern beginnt – zu einem visuellen Spiel der Auflösung bei.
So gesehen kann man mancherorts von einem räumlichen Striptease sprechen. Alexandra Bircken lässt in ihrem Werk kaum einen Topos aus, der nicht der symbolischen Ordnung des Weiblichen zuzuordnen wäre, sowohl betreffend kultureller Verweissysteme, ebenso aber – und dies ist die logische Konsequenz – bezüglich kunsthistorischer Referenzen, die sich ausgehend von eben diesen gesellschaftlichen Fragestellungen entwickelten. Während also ein in der Luft hängendes Fadengespinst von Eva Hesse (*Right After,* 1969) ein Netz der Absenz suggerierte, das Prozess, Bewegung, Fragilität und flexible Form bejahte, nutzt Bircken vierzig Jahre später ebensolche Netze mit offenkundiger Selbstverständlichkeit und reichert sie mit Dingen an, die in ihrem Alltag gestrandet sind. Sie zeigt keinerlei Berührungsängste zum Handgemachten und Dekorativen, sie entlehnt vieles nicht nur der Mode, sondern auch dem Bereich des Häuslichen: Hängende Tragsysteme und das Mobile tauchen auf (*Not Ikea,* 2009, *Soulution,* 2010), Wäscheaufhänger oder Bügelbretter werden als Tragestruktur Teil der Plastiken (*Not Beyond Repair,* 2008), Spielsachen wie Lego, Schaukelpferd oder Skateboard dienen ihr als Ansatzpunkte, sie räumlich fortzuspinnen (*Containerland,* 2010, *Chariot,* 2012). Genannt seien auch die zahlreichen Raumkonstruktionen, die sich an unterschiedlichen Behausungsformen orientieren (*Porthole,* 2009, *Quelle,* 2011, *Cagey,* 2012). Die Figur der Frau selbst platziert Bircken mancherorts in Form von Schaufensterpuppen. *Beinahe* (2010) besteht aus Mannequinbeinen, die, in einen purpurroten Sockel aus Wachs eingelassen, anstelle eines Bauchs ein auf dem Kopf stehendes Puppenhaus aufweisen. Dieses scheint ähnlich gefährlich auf dem Satteldach zu kippeln, wie der verführerisch rote Lippenstift die Erwartungen in einen Frauenbauch aus dem Gleichgewicht bringen kann. Bircken spielt visuell die Begriffspaare „Bauch" und „Puppenhaus", „Lippenstift" und „Sockel aus Wachs" virtuos gegeneinander aus, um „Frau" und „Haus" zu „Hausfrau" ebenso wie „Frauenhaus" zu verweben. Was mich an dieser Stelle dazu führt, daran zu

erinnern, dass wichtige Eckpunkte in der Geschichte der so genannten „feministischen Kunst" genau mit diesen Begriffen bestritten wurden: *Womanhouse,* eine für die feministische Kunst legendär gewordene installative Ausstellung und Performance, die 1972 von Judy Chicago und Miriam Schapiro initiiert wurde, beinhaltete ein Werk namens *Dollhouse.*[7]

Das Terrain des Feminismus

Unweigerlich betreten wir das Terrain des heute so schwer auszusprechenden Begriffs des Feminismus. „Sich heute als Frau zu identifizieren, bedeutet vor allem, in eine alte Opferrolle zu schlüpfen", so Gertrud Koch in einem Statement zum Feminismus heute.[8] Bezogen auf die Kunst haben sich viele Künstlerinnen von An-beginn gegen feministische Ansätze ausgesprochen, denn die Gefahr liegt nahe, ein Werk verkürzt und einge-engt zu rezipieren. Bridget Riley schimpfte den heutigen Feminismus die „Hysterie des 19. Jahrhunderts" und stellte die Begrifflichkeit einem künstlerischen Todesurteil gleich.[9] An der Ambivalenz der Kategorie hat sich bisher nichts geändert, zumal sie heute mit ihrer historischen Patina gerne für veraltet gehalten wird und in der Debatte der letzten Jahrzehnte an Komplexität gewonnen hat. Während selbstverständlich von einer Tradition der Konzeptkunst gesprochen werden kann, ist weiterhin Vorsicht geboten, wenn nur ein Hauch von so etwas wie Feminismus (bekanntlich gibt es derer vieler) im Raum steht. So kommt es, dass wir heute das Wort kaum mehr aussprechen, das Bedürfnis, darüber zu verhandeln, besteht weiterhin – ein Blick in die Tagespresse genügt.[10] Wie ist es anders zu erklären, dass bisher in kaum einem Text über das Werk von Alexandra Bircken ihr nicht zu übersehender Reflex auf die heutige Lebensrealität der Frauen zur Sprache kommt? Wie kommt es, dass es kaum jemand wagt, über das Stichwort „Mode" hinaus, wenigstens im Ansatz ein ironisches Augenzwinkern auf die möglichen Lehren oder auch den Ballast des historischen Feminismus in die Diskussion einzuwerfen? Ist es nicht symptomatisch, dass noch bei Künstlerinnen wie Rosemarie Trockel oder Cindy Sherman durchaus feministische Anliegen besprochen wurden, bei Künst-lerinnen jüngerer Generation wie Bircken davor zurückgeschreckt wird?

Warum eigentlich fällt es noch immer schwer, Begriffe zu finden, welche eine künstlerische Haltung benennen, in der weibliche Lebenserfahrungen eine Rolle spielen? Peggy Phelan plädiert heute für die begriffliche Trennung von Kunst und Feminismus, die in ihrer Verbindung performative wie transformative Eigenschaf-ten annehmen: „Following [John Langshaw] Austin, art can be understood as a specific kind of action and feminism as a specific form of language. The promise of feminist art is the performative creation of new realities. Successful feminist art beckons us towards possibilities in thought and in practice still to be created, still to be lived."[11] Phelans unaufgeregte Analyse ist, wie ich finde, brauchbar, um die Größe „Feminismus" in die Debatte einzuführen, ohne sogleich alte Fronten (zwischen den Geschlechtern ebenso wie zwischen Frauen selbst) aufbrechen zu lassen. Unabhängig davon, wie Emanzipation auszusehen hätte, oder ob sie abgeschlossen sei oder nicht, bleibt die Frage im Raum, warum es nicht legitim und wichtig ist, weibliche Lebenserfahrung in der Kunst reflektiert zu wissen.[12]

Alexandra Birckens Werk fordert alle diese Fragen heraus, indem sie abermals die historisch verankerten Bilder des Weiblichen beharrlich und mit Vehemenz aufnimmt. Sie setzt sich dabei den oben skizzierten „Gefahren" aus und muss sich auch die Frage gefallen lassen, ob sie mit der Thematisierung von Stereotypen nicht dazu beiträgt, dasjenige, was kritisiert werden soll, gerade zu zementieren (eine Argumentationslinie, die den Feminismus stets begleitete). Wenn Bircken die klassisch verankerten Bilder des Weiblichen heute neuerlich aufgreift, trifft sie allerdings andere Pointen, als wenn sie dies vor fünfzig Jahren getan hätte. Denn einige Topoi erscheinen uns heute vor dem Hintergrund der immerhin langsam fortschreitenden Erosion klassischer Rollenverteilungen als überzeichnete Karikaturen. Auch damit spielt Bircken. Andere Aspekte jedoch, und hier sind besonders die psychoanalytisch verankerten Muster gemeint, dürften weiterhin das grundlegende Selbstverständnis jedes Einzelnen ansprechen. Bircken befeuert mit ihren verwebten Konglo-meraten im Raum emphatisch die machtvolle, erratische Kraft, die Freud in der Korrelation von Trieb und

27

Sublimation, von Weiblichem und dem Weben festmachte: „Man meint, dass die Frauen zu den Entdeckungen und Erfindungen der Kulturgeschichte wenig Beiträge geleistet haben, aber vielleicht haben sie doch eine Technik erfunden, die des Flechtens und Webens. Wenn dem so ist, so wäre man versucht, das unbewusste Motiv dieser Leistung zu erraten. Die Natur selbst hätte das Vorbild für diese Nachahmung gegeben, indem sie mit der Geschlechtsreife die Genitalbehaarung wachsen ließ, die das Genital verhüllt."[13] Gerade die psychoanalytische Dimension, die dem Weben inhärent ist und die Grund für so viele webende Protagonistinnen in der Kulturgeschichte ist, macht Bircken für sich fruchtbar.[14]

Obschon Freud eine machtvolle Potenz dem Weiblichen zuschrieb, macht das Zitat die seiner Zeit inhärente patriarchale Voreingenommenheit deutlich. Bircken verkehrt die Ressentiments in ihrem konsequenten Rekurs auf thematische wie kunsthistorische Aspekte, die sie aus dem Erbe der feministischen Kunst schöpft, ins Gegenteil: Sie zelebriert Heldinnen – in Form der Frau per se ebenso wie in Form von Reminiszenzen an Werke vorgängiger Künstlerinnen. Schließlich gehört sie einer der ersten Generationen an, denen es möglich ist, auf ein substantielles künstlerisches Erbe von Frauen rekurrieren zu können. Indem Bircken die Chiffren der historischen feministischen Kunst systematisch wiederbelebt, öffnet sie uns das Auge für den heute blinden Fleck, nämlich unsere zaghafte Auseinandersetzung mit dem Feminismus. Tatsache ist, dass ihr Werk mich bewogen hat, die Begrifflichkeit aus dem Dunst des Impliziten zum Expliziten zu machen. Niemand wird bestreiten wollen, dass unser Dasein, Verstehen und Gehen in die Welt weiterhin – und zum Glück – sehr wohl geschlechtlich geprägt ist. Es lohnt, sich mit Bircken lustvoll auf Höhenflüge zu schwingen: In *Icarus Survivor* (2009) hat sie dem Übermütigen eine signalrote Rettungsweste verpasst – wir stürzen mit Bircken nicht ab, vielmehr werden wir ermuntert, zu Vorstellungswelten nahe der Sonne aufzubrechen. Im schlimmsten Fall tauchen wir ins kühle Nass, aber wir müssen uns nicht unterkriegen lassen, mit Rettungsweste gehen wir nicht verloren.

1: Im englischen Original erschienen als Sylvia Plath: The Bell Jar, London 1966, Erstveröffentlichung 1963 unter dem Pseudonym Victoria Lucas. Die Autorin wurde posthum zu einer Ikone der Frauenbewegung.

2: Louise Bourgeois in dem Interview: Alles ist möglich in New York, Kulturzeit extra, 3Sat 2005, www.3sat.de/page/?source=/kulturzeit/specials/86947/index.html, letzter Zugriff: 18.12.2012.

3: Im Titel *Uknit* spielt Alexandra Bircken mit den Bedeutungen von englisch „you knit" und „unite".

4: Seth Siegelaub (Hg.): Bibliographica Textilia Historiae. Towards a General Bibliography on the History of Textiles Based on the Library and Archives of the Center for Social Research on Old Textiles, New York 1997, S. 9.

5: Nina Felshin: „Clothing as subject", in: Art Journal, Vol. 54, No. 1, New York 1995, S. 20. Vgl. weiterführend Cora von Pape: Kunstkleider. Die Präsenz des Körpers in textilen Kunst-Objekten des 20. Jahrhunderts, Bielefeld 2008.

6: Vgl. Abbildungen S. 102–105.

7: Vgl. Helena Reckitt (Hg.): Art and Feminism, London 2012. Die Korrelation Frau und Haus hat zahlreiche Künstler beschäftigt, insbesondere möchte ich auf die Reihe *Femme Maison* von Louise Bourgeois hinweisen, in der jeweils der Kopf der Frau durch ein Haus ersetzt wird. Bourgeois hat dieses Motiv in unterschiedlichen Medien, Zeichnung, Malerei und Plastik, umgesetzt.

8: Gertrud Koch: „Feminismus nach der Identitätspolitik", in: Isabelle Graw (Hg.): Feminismus!, Texte zur Kunst Nr. 84, Dezember 2011, S. 68–71.

9: Vgl. dem Essay vorangestelltes Zitat von Bridget Riley, eine Äußerung der Künstlerin zur Rolle der Frauenbewegung in ihrer Kunst. Ausführlicher nachzulesen bei Élisabeth Lebovici: „Women's art: What's in a name?", in: Camille Morineau (Hg.): elles@centrepompidou. Women artists in the collection of the Musée National d'Art moderne de création industrielle, Ausst.Kat. Centre Pompidou, Paris 2009, S. 279. Georgia O'Keeffe wehrte sich zeitlebens gegen die Behauptung, sie sei eine feministische Künstlerin. Ihr Werk wurde sowohl in den 20er Jahren wie auch in den 70er Jahren gerne unter feministischen Gesichtspunkten besprochen, u. a. wurden ihre Blumenmotive als Vulva-Formen diskutiert. Vgl. Barbara Buhler Lynes: „Georgia O'Keeffe and Feminism: A Problem of Position", in: Norma Broude, Mary Garrard (Hg.): The Expanding Discourse: Feminism and Art History, New York 1992, S. 437–450.

10: Es ist um ein Vielfaches leichter, feministische künstlerische Haltungen in der Historie zu konsolidieren und auf ihre Erfolge hinzuweisen, als gegenwärtige, weiterführende Stimmen zu diskutieren. In den vergangenen Jahren sind entsprechend zahlreiche Ausstellungen, Symposien und Publikationen zum Thema erschienen, allerdings standen dabei die Geschichte des Feminismus und eine Revision der Institutionspolitik der Museen stärker im Fokus als neue künstlerische Impulse der Gegenwart. Vgl. Lisa Gabrielle Mark (Hg.): Wack! Art and the Feminist Revolution, Ausst.Kat. Museum of Contemporary Art Los Angeles, Cambridge/London 2007; Cornelia Butler, Alexandra Schwartz (Hg.): Modern Women. Women Artists at the Museum of Modern Art, Ausst.Kat. MoMA New York, New York 2010; Camille Morineau (Hg.): elles@centrepompidou. Women artists in the collection of the Musée National d'Art moderne de création industrielle, Ausst.Kat. Centre Pompidou, Paris 2009; Die andere Seite des Mondes. Künstlerinnen der Avantgarde, Ausst.Kat. Kunstsammlung Nordrhein-Westfalen, Düsseldorf 2012.

11: Peggy Phelan: „Survey", in: Helena Reckitt (Hg.): Art and Feminism, London 2006, S. 20. Zahlreiche Umschwünge sind in der Debatte um den Feminismus nachzuzeichnen: angefangen bei oft im Kollektiv verfolgten Dekonstruktionen des patriarchalen Systems in den 60er Jahren, über

einen Essentialismus, der stark von der Psychoanalyse geprägt nach spezifisch weiblichen Denkformen und Herangehensweisen („écriture féminine")
suchte, bis hin zu den 90er Jahren, in denen das Instabile und Flexible im Verständnis der Geschlechter im Zentrum stand und auf diese Weise den
Feminismus gewissermaßen in die Gender Studies aufgehen ließ.

12: In vielerlei Hinsicht ist es heute für Männer einfacher über Feminismus zu sprechen als für Frauen, denn während der Mann damit Aufge-
schlossenheit suggeriert, läuft die Frau beim Sprechen über dieselben Inhalte Gefahr, sich im Sinne von Koch in die Opferrolle zu begeben, und muss
sich den Vorwurf gefallen lassen, in altbackene Litanei zu verfallen oder gar weibliche Kumpanei zu betreiben. Zum gegenwärtigen Zwiespalt und
der zunehmenden Komplexität, der man im Umgang mit dem Feminismus begegnet, vgl. Monika Szewczyk: „Ein Flirt mit dem Feminismus", in:
Sophie Kaplan, Christina Végh, Janneke de Vries (Hg.): Shannon Bool. Inverted Harem, Ausst.Kat. Bonner Kunstverein, CRAC Alsace – Centre
Rhénan d'Art Contemporain, GAK Gesellschaft für aktuelle Kunst Bremen, Berlin 2011, S. 38–40.

13: Sigmund Freud: „Die Weiblichkeit", in: ders.: Neue Folge der Vorlesungen zur Einführung in die Psychoanalyse, 33. Vorlesung (1933),
Studienausgabe Bd. 1, Frankfurt a. M. 2000, S. 562.

14: Noch einmal verweise ich auf Louise Bourgeois, deren Mutter tatsächlich Weberin war und in deren Werk Netze (und Spinnen) für Ursprung
und Schutz stehen. „Meine Mutter war meine beste Freundin. Sie war klug, geduldig, tröstend, feinfühlig, fleißig, unentbehrlich und vor allem,
sie war eine Weberin – wie die Spinne." Louise Bourgeois in dem Interview: Alles ist möglich in New York, Kulturzeit extra, 3Sat 2005.

WEAVING

"At this point in time, artists who happen to be women need this particular form of hysteria like they need
a hole in the head." – Bridget Riley, 1972

Penelope

There are different reasons for pursuing the craft of weaving. Penelope wove in order to survive her long
years of waiting. While her husband Odysseus was venturing abroad, she was beset by numerous suitors
whom she could only hold at bay thanks to her guile. She made her availability as a bride dependent upon
completing her weaving, unpicking at night what she had created during the day. It takes many threads to
create a fine cloth – time, energy, history are woven into them. Alexandra Bircken often addresses the question
of how one particular thing can be connected to another, and yet how everything is somehow interconnected.
Her range of materials is all-embracing: natural things, remnants of abandoned birds' nests, branches, hair
or wax, materials such as wool, fabrics, rubber, as well as plastic, metal, found and recyclable objects alike
are all utilised. In her heterogeneous world of things, they have only one thing in common: the objects are
unmanageable, recalcitrant, difficult to mould and not originally intended to be sculptural elements. Bircken
integrates this worthless flotsam into her installations – her stretched support structures – arriving thus at
idiosyncratic, heterogeneous formations that coexist as hybrids in space, both as an abstract form and as a
reference system of a lived, popular culture.

Mrs. Willard

Weaving is a classic example of the symbolic order of the feminine. Mrs. Willard, a character in Sylvia Plath's
novel *The Bell Jar,* is preoccupied with weaving.[1] However, in this context, weaving represents futility rather
than a possible rescue or redemption. Mrs. Willard regularly made carpets out of her husband's old suits, only
to use them as doormats despite so much diligent labour, thereby surrendering them to inevitable wear and
tear. Much like Mrs. Willard, Bircken also often makes use of used textiles for her woven sculptures, but reverses
certain aspects, such as fragmentation and futility, into confidence and celebration. Her artistic approach is
akin to that of Louise Bourgeois, who describes it as follows: "I do something, I destroy it, I do it again and
I always come back to it. It is a privilege to sublimate. Many people cannot sublimate. They don't have any
access to their unconscious."[2]
Bircken's exhibitions have titles such as *Blondie* or *Hausrat* [Household Stuff], her works are presented as
Twiggy (2012) or, as in the case of *Uknit Bonn* (2012), they wittily challenge us both to knit and to congregate.[3]

29

We can talk of guile here, too, when Bircken reclaims these quintessentially stereotypical connotations and restages such classically traditional symbols in all their clarity. Haven't we heard it so many times before? We know: women knit and weave and it behoves them to join forces, they love soft fabrics and things made by hand, they care about coverings and relationships, and yet they are, after all, in demand in recent times in the labour market thanks to their highly developed social competence. Bircken animates these classical ideas by systematically restaging them, by installing them theatrically in space and allowing the viewer to engage with both a cheerful yet dramatic mise en scène. We find ourselves enmeshed in a skein of dense, ambiguous webs and networks until we are finally convinced that the professor or bank manager is a "blonde", that the powerful control centre, that place of knowledge and the production of money, is in fact surrounded by domestic paraphernalia, that the suit is in fact a "Twiggy" and that knitting – not smartphones – is the order of the day.

Christopher Columbus

It is not just weaving as an activity, but textiles per se that are assigned to the domain of the female. Accordingly, there are a number of prominent female artists who devote themselves to the amorphous, to materials that shroud and protect the human form. Down the years, in the history of art it was the masterful (male) task to elevate the drape of fabric from the depths of patent handcraft to the heights of fine art, be it on canvas or in marble. Fabric, which in itself has no form, but conforms and cleaves to its mould, has only entered the material inventory of art since the late 1960s in the shape of postminimalist tendencies, such as "eccentric abstraction" or "anti-form". It is well known that it was predominantly female artists who contributed crucially to these new forms of sculpture. Consequently, it is amazing that textiles and weaving were considered to be inferior for such a long time, particularly when one considers the huge impact of this cultural achievement, which, for its part, extends into our modern digital and global world. Seth Siegelaub, a conceptual art theorist and expert on the history of weaving, establishes a connection between Christopher Columbus as a scion of weavers and other portentous achievements of the human race: "The intimate relationship between textiles and society can also be seen in the fundamental role it played in the rise of the capitalist system, as the first large-scale capitalist industry (the production and export of wool in medieval Flanders); in the industrial revolution (the mechanization of cotton spinning and weaving in eighteenth-century England); in architecture, as the object of the first multi-storied iron frame building (Bage's flax mill in Shrewsbury, England in 1796); as the subject of the first working-class history (Henson's history of the framework-knitters in 1831); or as the subject of the first semiotic text (Roland Barthes, La Mode, Paris 1963); not to mention that the French word for loom is the same as the general word for profession or trade ('métier'), and the German word for textiles is the same as the general word for material or matter ('Stoffe'), which is also the case for the Dutch word 'stof', as well as in English, with the word 'material'. [...] Perhaps it is by chance that Christopher Columbus, like his father, was first a wool weaver and wool merchant, but it is quite logical that the Jacquard loom in early nineteenth-century France was the inspiration for the work of Charles Babbage in England which led directly to the invention of the computer in the twentieth century."[4]

Bircken is likewise interested in the structure of textiles, which has been so significant both culturally and historically for many developments in other areas of life. Each fabric and each weave consists of a plurality of individual, enmeshed elements (again, the idea of community is evident here!) that can only work when taken in their entirety. Moreover, we are always dealing with mobile, stretchable, more or less flexible and variable weaves: sewn on to wall coverings, nylon stockings with lace and gussets are stretched out patchwork-like and mutate into animal skins – renowned as hunting trophies and the place holders of virile potency (*Skin 2*, 2010). Bircken's nylons remain seductive – both in their purpose as a garment, as well as within an artwork – and at the same time, they appear as the skin of a dangerous animal that Columbus might well have encountered in the New World. As a logical consequence, there are also other "remnants" of fallen prey: *Knochen* [Bones] (2011) or scalp-like formations (*Pamela Combat*, 2010, a joint work with Thomas Brinkmann). Naturally, Bircken, not unlike Columbus (or Adam) on her artistic journey, investigates the exotic or forbidden fruit with its libidinous flesh (*Bundle*, 2007, *What is this*, 2008), nor does she shy away from spectral demons (*Tentakel* [Tentacle], 2009).

Garments for Rooms, the Dressing and Undressing of Spaces

Bircken, who originally studied fashion design and whose work can be understood as a kind of pupation of this field, creates clothes for rooms and spaces without ever forgetting the adage that clothes maketh the man. "Clothing, more than any other object or possession, is closely identified with the body of the absent wearer."[5] *Bündel* [Bundle] (2009), for example, comprises found textiles and embroidered segments knitted and crocheted by the artist herself to create a floor sculpture, which stands there in the space resembling a footstool. It is possible to pick out sweaters or T-shirts here and there, duly deprived of their functions. They can be read as symbols of today and may also evoke images of human indigence, yet they also remain abstract form, pedestal and sculpture alike. Bircken uses the strong bond that exists between clothing and wearer when she lines the space with textile structures: woven form literally inserts itself into the architecture as an abstract pattern in a kind of stretched system (*Insert,* 2009), or proffers itself as a surface keen to record events taking place within the space (*Receptor,* 2009). In *Uknit Bonn* (2012), once more Bircken uses metal to suggest mesh, cladding the entire length of a room. The martial reference to armour is turned on its head in the form of something hand-knitted, which is furnished with a row of mesh that quite literally seems to step out of line.[6] Here, too, concurrences are an integral part of the interpretation, because in addition to the cultural and socio-political implications, the formal, aesthetic considerations are always ever being addressed. The metallic dress reflects incidental light back into the room, thus contributing to a visual game of dissolution when the mesh area starts to flicker.

In this sense, one can almost speak of a spatial striptease here and there. Alexandra Bircken scarcely omits a single topos from her work that could be assigned to the symbolic order of the feminine, not only in terms of cultural reference systems, but likewise – and this is the logical consequence – with regard to art historical references, which in turn developed on the basis of these very social issues. So while Eva Hesse's suspended, tangled web (*Right After*, 1969) suggested a network of absence yet simultaneously affirmed process, movement, fragility and flexible form, Bircken, some forty years later, uses the selfsame matrices with blatant self-evidence and enriches them with the flotsam and jetsam of her everyday life. She does not fear the handmade and decorative, she borrows much not only from the world of fashion, but also from the domestic domain: suspended support systems and mobiles are featured (*Not Ikea*, 2009, *Soulution*, 2010), laundry racks and ironing boards are used as support structures for the sculptures (*Not Beyond Repair*, 2008), toys such as Lego, a rocking horse or skateboard serve her as a springboard for the continued spatial fabulation of her themes (*Containerland*, 2010, *Chariot,* 2012). Worthy of mention here are the numerous configurations of space based on different types of dwelling (*Porthole*, 2009, *Source*, 2011, *Cagey*, 2012). Here and there, Bircken uses the mannequin to represent woman as a figure. *Beinahe* [Almost] (2010) consists of a pair of mannequin's legs, inserted in a purple wax base or pedestal, and in place of the womb, we see an upside-down doll's house.[7] Similarly, this seems to be teetering dangerously on its gable roof, in the same way that the seductive red lipstick can destabilise the expectations inherent in a woman's womb. Bircken visually pits the conceptual pairs "womb" and "doll's house", "lipstick" and "wax pedestal" against each other in virtuoso fashion, in order to interweave the motifs "wife" and "home" with "housewife" and "women's refuge". At which point, I cannot but recall that the significant milestones in the history of so-called "feminist art" were contested in precisely these terms: *Womanhouse*, a legendary installation exhibition and performance in the annals of feminist art, initiated in 1972 by Judy Chicago and Miriam Schapiro, contained an artwork entitled *Dollhouse*.[8]

The Terrain of Feminism

Inevitably we are now entering the terrain of feminism, a term that is so difficult to utter nowadays. To identify oneself as a woman today means, above all, "to slip into an old, established victim role", as Gertrud Koch puts it in a statement about feminism today.9 In the case of art, many artists have expressed opposition to feminist approaches from the outset, because of the obvious danger of narrowing down and concentrating the reception of the work in question. Bridget Riley chided today's feminism as "nineteenth-century hysteria" and effectively sounded an artistic death knell for the concept.10 Nothing about the ambivalent nature of the category has changed, especially since it is readily considered obsolete today with its somewhat historical patina, and the debate has also grown in complexity over recent decades. Whereas one can speak confidently about a tradition in conceptual art, it is still necessary to exercise caution when only a mere hint of something like feminism – there are many, as is well known – is mentioned. So it has come to pass that we hardly ever utter the word today, yet the need to negotiate its parameters abides nonetheless – a brief glimpse at the daily papers suffices to confirm this.11 How else can one explain that, so far, texts on Alexandra Bircken scarcely ever mention the indisputable reaction to today's reality for women so clearly manifest in her work? How can it be that hardly anyone – venturing beyond the keyword "fashion" – dares to introduce into the discussion at least an ironic nod to the possible lessons learned or the ballast of historical feminism? Is it not symptomatic that when artists, such as Cindy Sherman and Rosemarie Trockel are discussed, key feminist issues are inevitably integral to the debate, yet when it comes to younger artists such as Bircken, the tendency is to shy away from the matter?

Why is it still so difficult to find terminology which describes an artistic attitude in which women's life experiences play a role? Today, Peggy Phelan calls for the conceptual separation of art and feminism, which, when combined, assume both performative and transformative properties: "Following [John Langshaw] Austin, art can be understood as a specific kind of action and feminism as a specific form of language. The promise of feminist art is the performative creation of new realities. Successful feminist art beckons us towards possibilities in thought and in practice still to be created, still to be lived."12 Phelan's unemotional analysis is, I think, useful when introducing the colossus "feminism" into the debate, without necessarily reviving old antagonisms (between the sexes and between women themselves). Regardless of the form emancipation might take, or whether indeed it has been successfully implemented or not, the question remains of why it is not deemed legitimate or important that female life experience should be reflected in art.13

Alexandra Bircken's work poses all these challenging questions by persistently and vehemently readopting historically anchored images of the female. In so doing, she exposes herself to the "risks" outlined hitherto and must put up with the question of whether the thematic focus upon stereotypes in fact contributes to a cementing of the very thing that is being critiqued in the first place or not (a line of argument that has continually accompanied feminism). If today, Bircken is readopting the classical core images of the female, she delivers altogether different punchlines from the ones she might have delivered fifty years ago. For certain topoi appear to us today to be exaggerated caricatures in the light of the admittedly slow, yet nonetheless progressive erosion of traditional roles. Bircken plays on this, too. However, other aspects, and what is particularly meant here are those psychoanalytically rooted patterns, are still likely to address the fundamental self-understanding of every individual. Bircken, with her woven spatial conglomerations, emphatically fuels the powerful, erratic force that Freud identified in the correlation between drive and sublimation, between the female and weaving: "It is held that women have made few contributions to the discoveries and inventions in our civilisation, but maybe they have invented a technique, namely that of plaiting and weaving. If so, one might be tempted to speculate about the unconscious motive of this performance. Nature itself would seem to have provided the model which this achievement imitates by causing the growth at puberty of the pubic hair that conceals the genitals."14 Bircken avails herself in particular of the fruitful psychoanalytical dimension which is inherent in weaving and is responsible for the profusion of protagonists in cultural history who also weave.15

Although Freud ascribed a powerful potency to the feminine, his observation clearly highlights the inherent, patriarchal prejudices of his time. Bircken reverses the polarity of resentment operating in her systematic recourse to thematic and art historical aspects, which she draws from the legacy of feminist art: she celebrates heroines –

in the form of women per se, as well as in the form of her revisitations to the work of her female artist predecessors. Ultimately, she belongs to one of the first generations able to have recourse to a substantial female artistic legacy. By systematically resurrecting the codes of historic feminist art, Bircken opens our eyes to this current blind spot, namely our tentative engagement with feminism. In fact, her work has prompted me to shift my terms of reference here from the diffusely implicit to the explicit. Thankfully, no one will deny that our existence, our understanding, our comings and goings in the world will continue to be shaped by and through gender. It is most definitely worthwhile to join Bircken in her joyful, high-altitude flights of fancy: in *Icarus Survivor* (2009), she has dressed the hubristic protagonist in a bright red life jacket – we won't plunge to earth with Bircken, instead we are encouraged to journey on to imaginary worlds close to the sun. At worst, we'll end up all wet in the cold water, but we shouldn't allow ourselves to be defeated – we have our life jackets, we are not lost.

1: Sylvia Plath, *The Bell Jar* (London, 1966). First published in 1963 under the pseudonym Victoria Lucas. The authoress became a posthumous icon of the women's movement.

2: Louise Bourgeois in the interview: "Alles ist möglich in New York", *Kulturzeit extra*, 3Sat 2005, www.3sat.de (last accessed: 6.12.12).

3: The title *Uknit* is clearly a play on "you knit" and "unite".

4: Seth Siegelaub, ed., *Bibliographica Textilia Historiae. Towards a General Bibliography on the History of Textiles Based on the Library and Archives of the Center for Social Research on Old Textiles* (New York, 1997), p. 9.

5: Nina Felshin, "Clothing as subject", in: *Art Journal*, vol. 54, 1, (New York, 1995), p. 20. For a continuation here, cf. Cora von Pape, *Kunstkleider. Die Präsenz des Körpers in textilen Kunst-Objekten des 20. Jahrhunderts* (Bielefeld, 2008).

6: Cf. illustr. pp. 102–105.

7: Cf. illustr. p. 62.

8: Cf. Helena Reckitt, ed., *Art and Feminism* (London, 2012). The correlation between female and house has preoccupied many an artist. I should like to refer in particular to Louise Bourgeois's series *Femme Maison* in which the woman's head is replaced successively by a house. Bourgeois has deployed this motif in a variety of media, such as drawing, painting and sculpture.

9: Gertrud Koch, "Feminismus nach der Identitätspolitik", in: Isabelle Graw, ed., *Feminismus!* Texte zur Kunst 84 (December, 2011), pp. 68–71.

10: Cf. the statement made by Bridget Riley quoted at the outset of this essay on the role of the women's movement in her art. For a more detailed discussion, cf. Élisabeth Lebovici: "Women's art: What's in a name?", in: Camille Morineau, ed., *elles@centrepompidou. Women artists in the collection of the Musée National d'Art moderne de création industrielle*, exhib. cat. Centre Pompidou (Paris, 2009), p. 279. Throughout her entire life, Georgia O'Keeffe denied the claim that she was a feminist artist. Her work was eagerly discussed from a feminist perspective, in both the 1920s as well as the 1970s; her flower motifs among other things were discussed in terms of their resemblance to the vulva, cf. Barbara Buhler Lynes, "Georgia O'Keeffe and Feminism: A Problem of Position", in: Norma Broude, Mary Garrard, eds., *The Expanding Discourse: Feminism and Art History* (New York, 1992), pp. 437–450.

11: It is easier by far to consolidate feminist artistic attitudes in history and to indicate their successes than to discuss contemporary, developing voices. In recent years, numerous exhibitions, symposia and publications have appeared on the subject, but the history of feminism and a revision of the institutional policy of museums was more the subject of focus than contemporary new artistic impulses. Cf. Lisa Gabrielle Mark, ed., *Wack! Art and the Feminist Revolution*, exhib. cat. Museum of Contemporary Art Los Angeles (Cambridge/London, 2007); Cornelia Butler, Alexandra Schwartz, eds., *Modern Women. Women Artists at the Museum of Modern Art*, exhib. cat. MoMA New York (New York, 2010); Camille Morineau, ed., *elles@centrepompidou. Women artists in the collection of the Musée National d'Art moderne de création industrielle*, exhib. cat. Centre Pompidou (Paris, 2009); *Die andere Seite des Mondes. Künstlerinnen der Avantgarde,* exhib. cat. Kunstsammlung Nordrhein-Westfalen (Düsseldorf, 2012).

12: Peggy Phelan, "Survey", in: Helena Reckitt, ed., *Art and Feminism* (London, 2006), p. 20. Numerous reversals can be traced in the debate surrounding feminism: from the deconstruction of the patriarchal system in the 1960s, often collectively pursued, via an essentialism heavily influenced by psychoanalysis according to specifically female forms of thinking and approaches ("écriture féminine"), all the way to the 1990s where an instability and flexibility in an understanding between the sexes occupied centre stage, thus allowing feminism to merge with "gender studies" to a certain degree.

13: In many ways it is easier today for men to talk about feminism than for women, because while the man is thus suggesting a degree of openness, the woman, when speaking about the same content, runs the risk of falling into the role of victim as per Koch's understanding of the concept, and has to endure the reproach that she is availing herself of an outmoded litany or even operating a kind of female chumminess. On the current conflict and growing complexity encountered when addressing feminism, cf. Monika Szewczyk, "Flirting with Feminism", in: Sophie Kaplan, Christina Végh, Janneke de Vries, ed., *Shannon Bool, Inverted Harem*, exhib. cat. Bonner Kunstverein, CRAC Alsace – Centre Rhénan d'Art Contemporain, GAK Gesellschaft für aktuelle Kunst Bremen (Berlin, 2011), pp. 12–14.

14: Sigmund Freud, "Die Weiblichkeit", in: id., *Neue Folge der Vorlesungen zur Einführung in die Psychoanalyse*, lecture No. 33 (1933), student edition, vol. 1 (Frankfurt a. M., 2000), p. 562.

15: I must refer to Louise Bourgeois once again, whose mother actually was a weaver and in whose work the web (and the spider) represents origin and protection. "My mother was my best friend. She was clever, patient, soothing, sensitive, hardworking, and indispensable and, above all, she was a weaver – like the spider." Louise Bourgeois in the interview: "Alles ist möglich in New York", *Kulturzeit extra*, 3Sat 2005.

Receptor, 2009

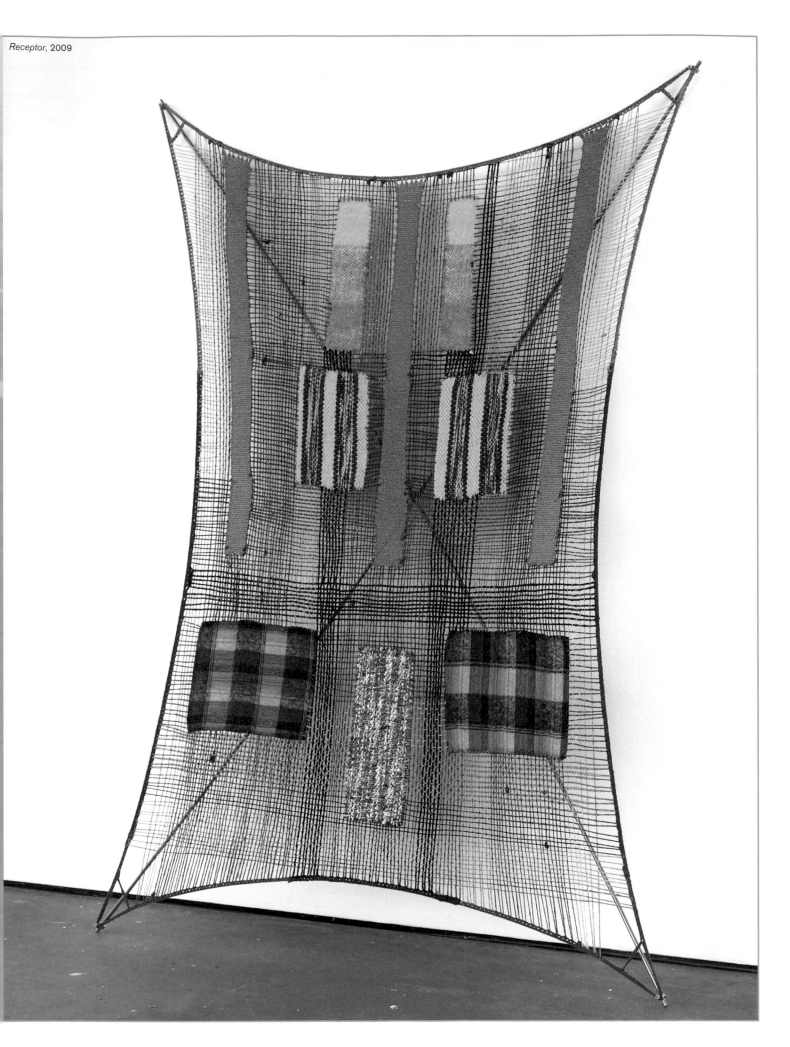

Icarus Survivor, 2009

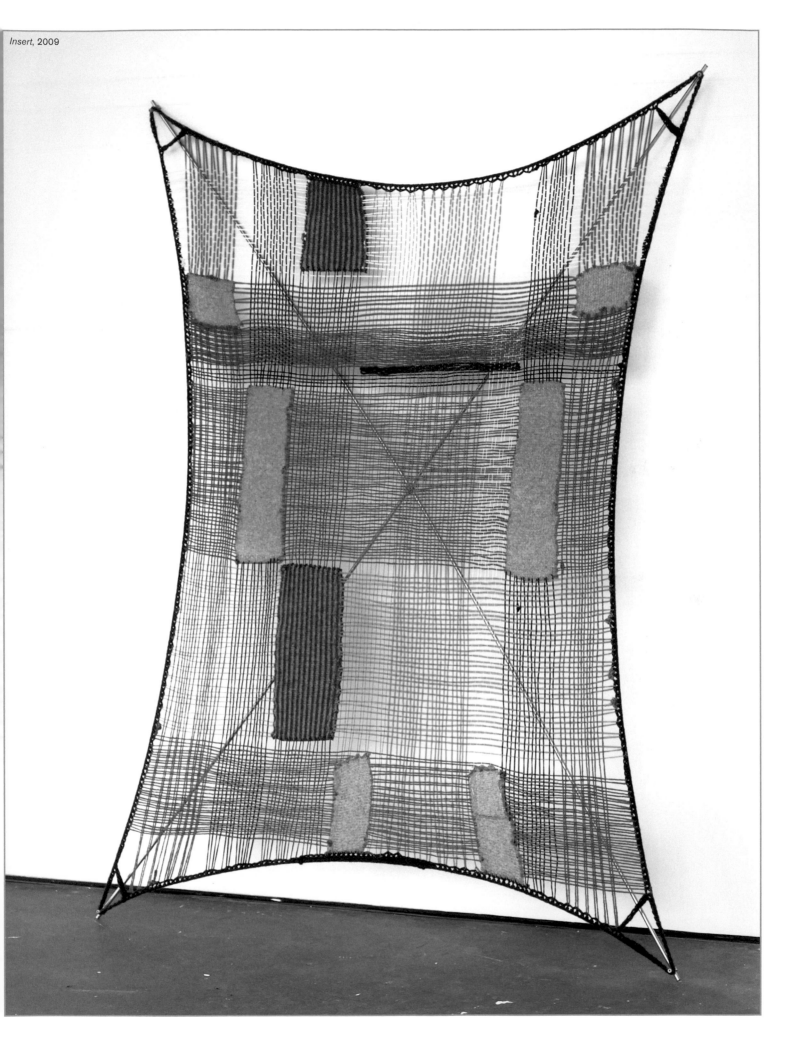

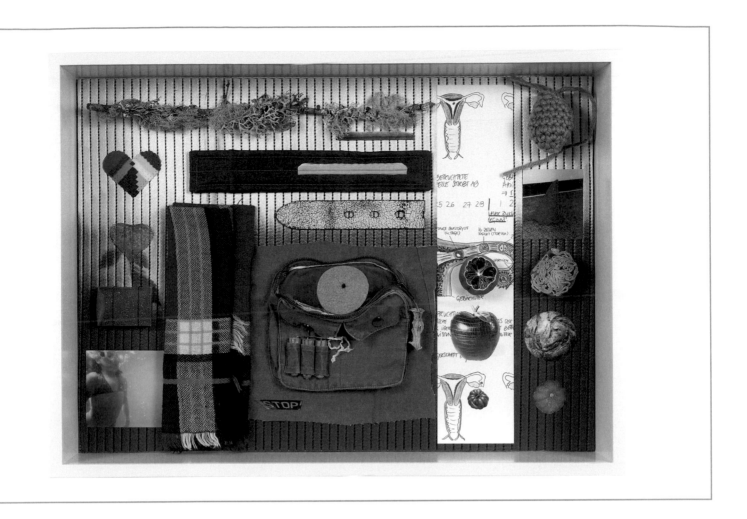

Thwack, 2009

Setup, 2009

5 O'Clock, 2009

Not Beyond Repair, 2008

Bundle, 2007

Was soll das, 2008

Porthole, 2009

Ensemble, 2008

Flaschengeist, 2008

Flaschengeist, 2008

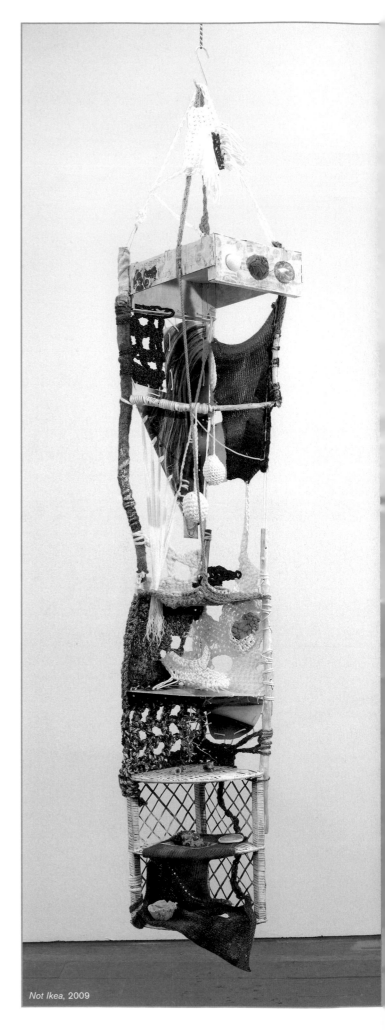

Not Ikea, 2009

Püppi auf Abwegen, 2009

Soulution, 2010

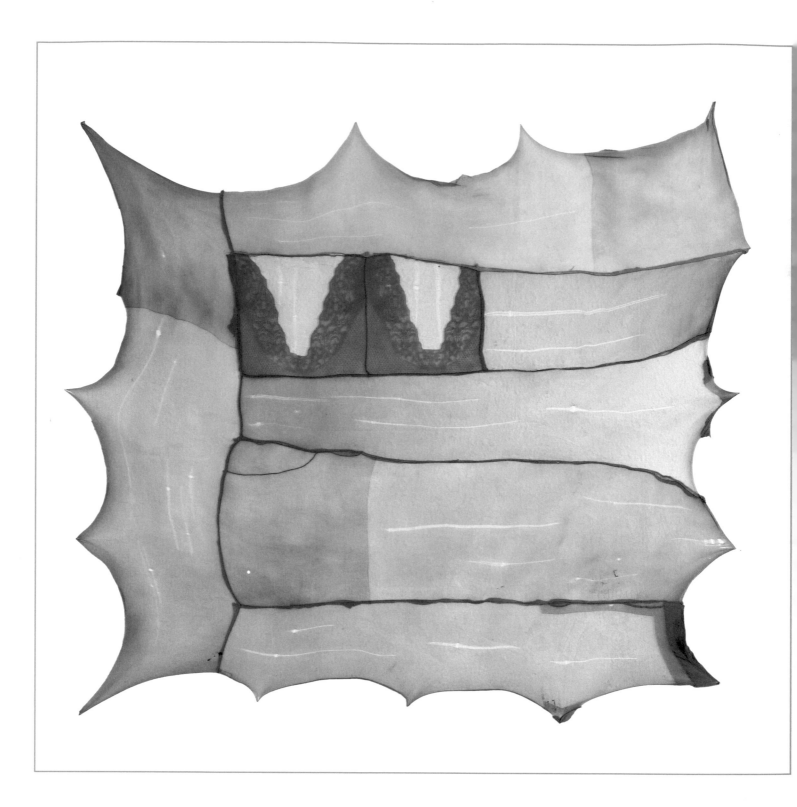

Skin 2, 2010

Lapsus, 2010

Take over, 2010

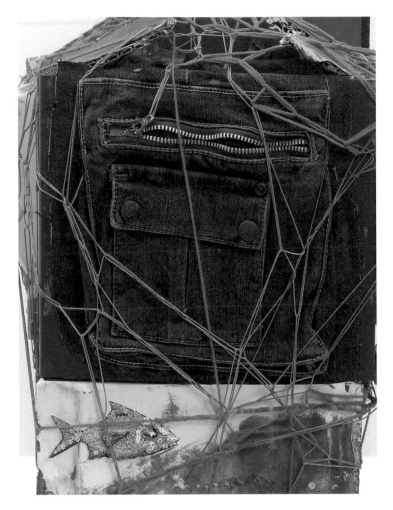

Containerland, 2009

Ohne Titel, 1991

Heart Core, 2011

Ohne Titel, 2011

Ganges, 2011

Fabrik, 2011

Knochen, 2011

Ship II, 2011

Womb, 2011

Cassius, 2011

8:9, 2011

In Mud I Trust, 2011

Puli, 2011

Runner in the Woods, 2011

Spinster, 2011

Alexandra Bircken und / and Thomas Brinkmann, *Twitter*, 2011

aHead IV, aHead III, aHead II, aHead I, 2011

Abyss, 2011

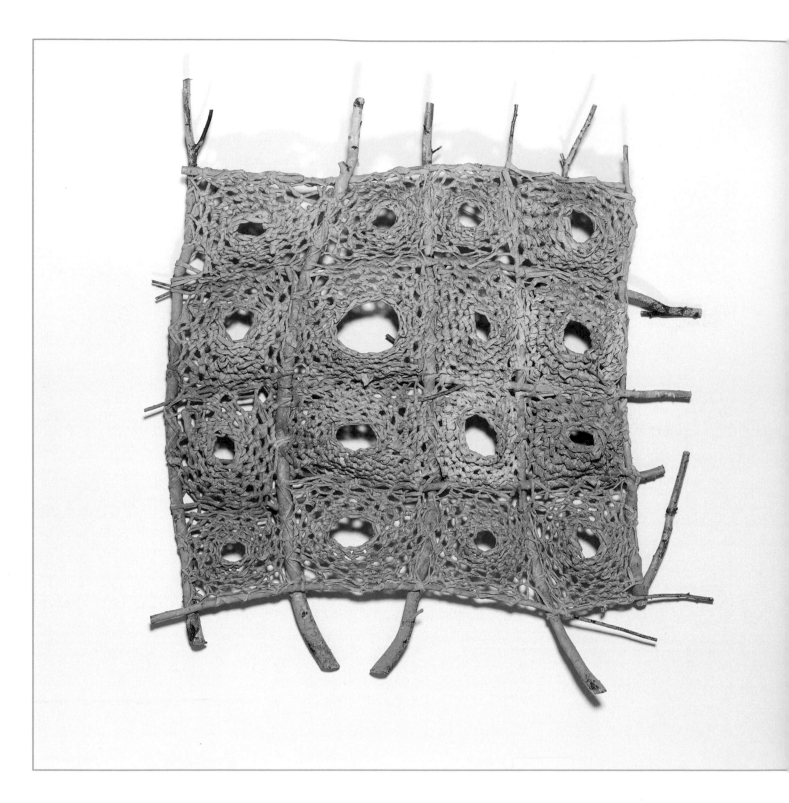

Birch Field, 2011

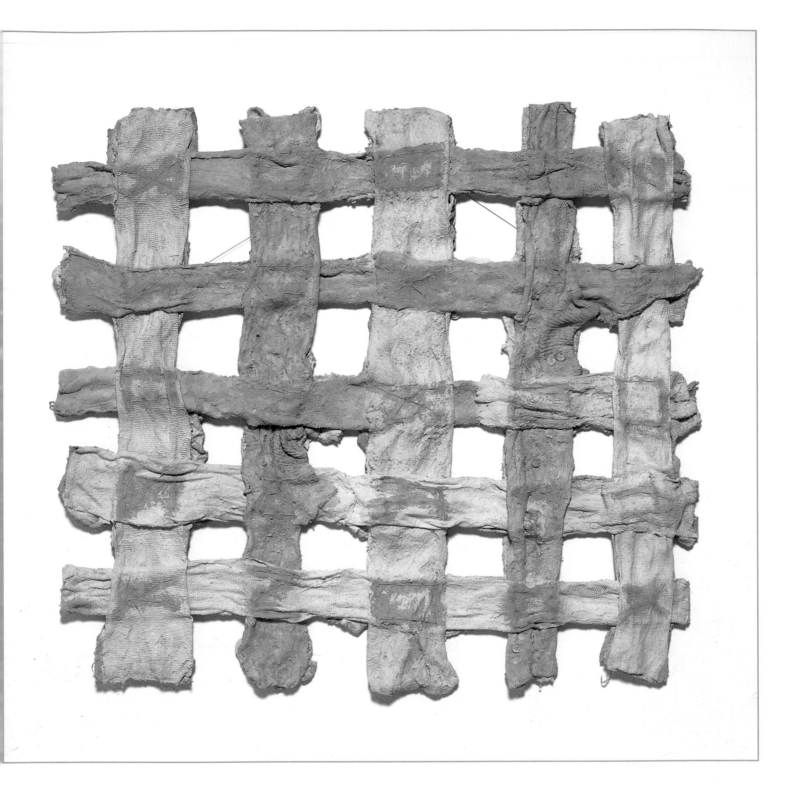

Extent, 2011

Black Skin, 2012

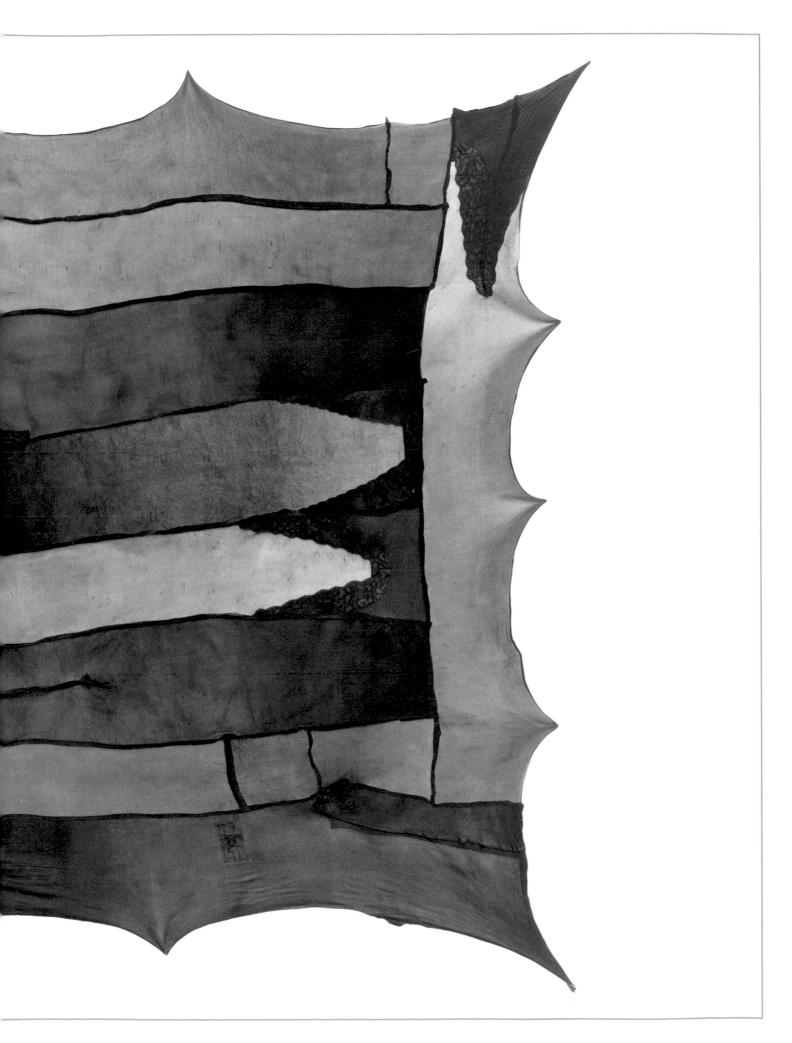

Uknit Bonn, 2012

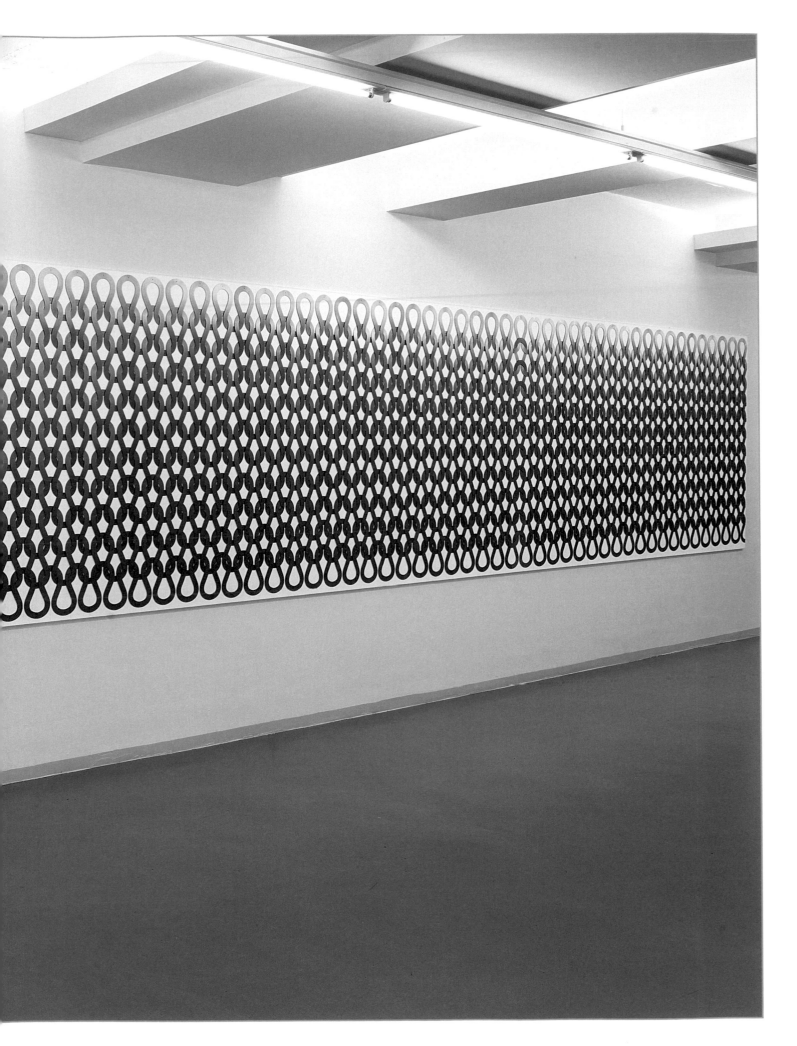

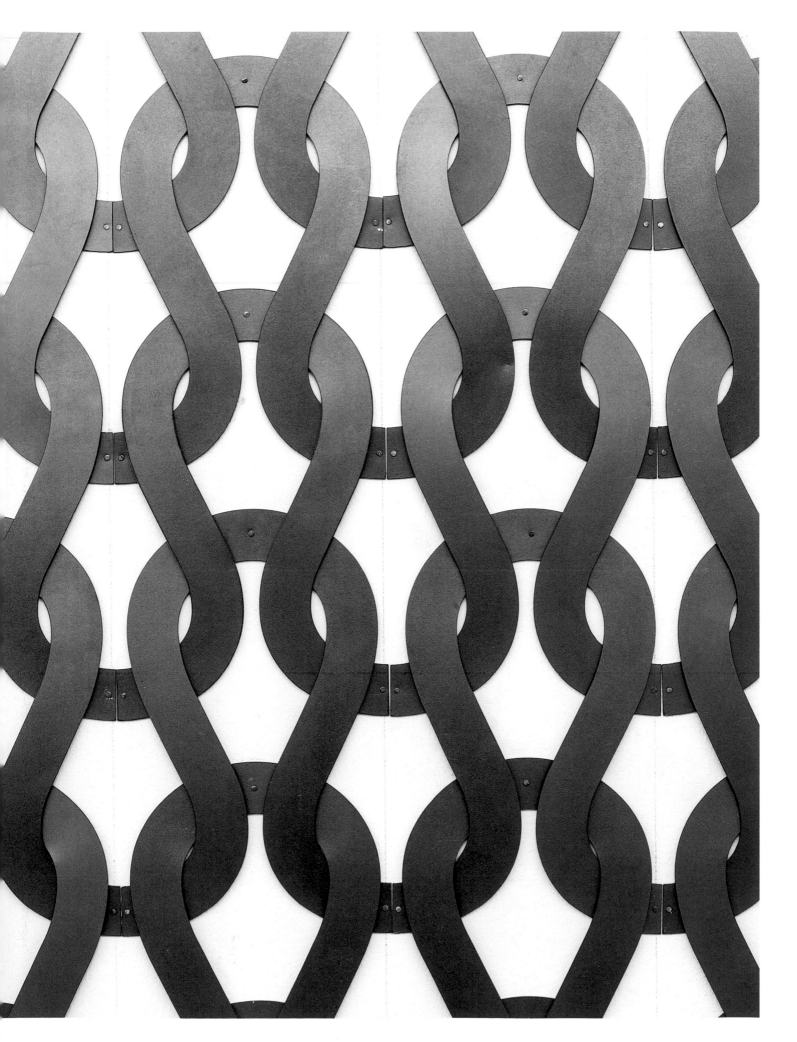

Cagey, 2012

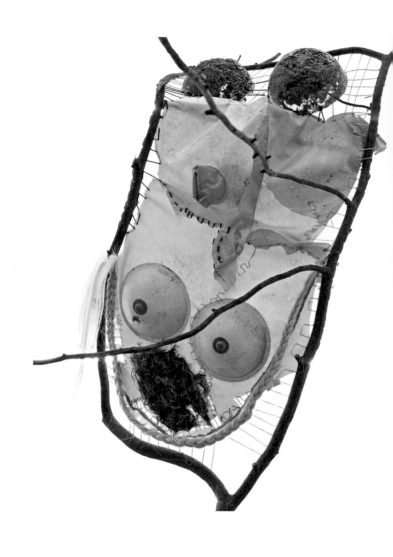

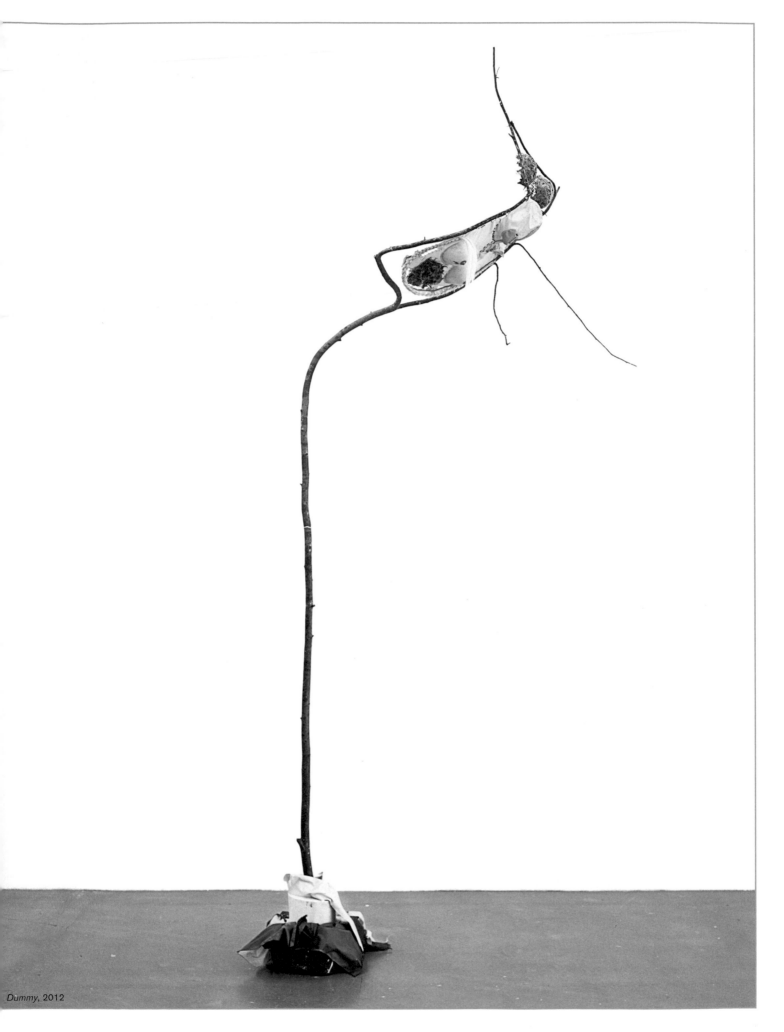

Dummy, 2012

DNA, 2012

Fadenheim, 2012

Koi, 2012

Eddie „The Eagle", 2012

Cheri Cheri Lady, 2012

Chariot, 2012

117

Twins, 2012

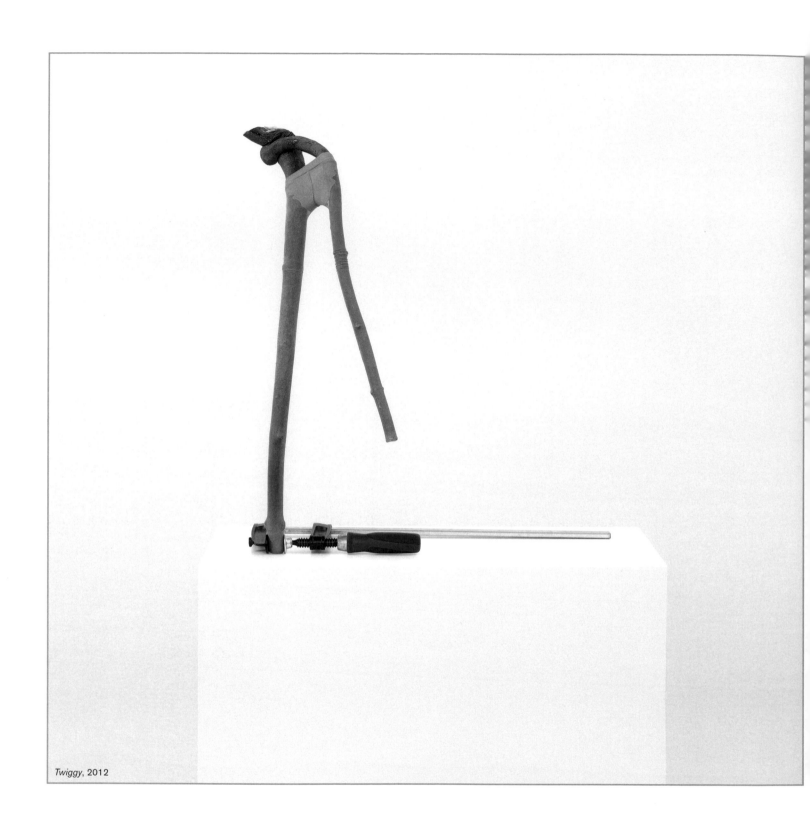

Twiggy, 2012

GiMoto, 2012

35
Receptor, 2009
Wolle, Fäden, Edelstahl, Elastic, Draht /
Wool, yarn, stainless steel, elastic, wire
220 x 164 x 16 cm
Privatsammlung / Private collection, Monaco

36
Icarus Survivor, 2009
Gips, Pigmente, Silber, Messing, Draht, Holz,
Sprühfarbe, Wolle, Weste, Hemd, Baumwolle,
Plastik, Klebstoff, Garn, Traubenstrunk /
Plaster, pigments, silver, brass, wire, wood,
metal, spraypaint, wool, waistcoat, shirt,
cotton, plastic, glue, thread, grape stem
140 x 138 x 24 cm
Kienbaum Collection Cologne

37
Insert, 2009
Wolle, Fäden, Edelstahl, Elastic, Draht /
Wool, yarn, stainless steel, elastic, wire
216 x 164 x 16 cm

38
Thwack, 2009
Gips, Farbe, Holz, Stoffe, Wolle, Haare,
Regenschirmhülle, verrostete Konservendose,
Pfirsichkern, Fotografien, Plastik, Wachs,
Metalle, Klebstoff, Garn / Plaster, paint, wood,
fabrics, wool, hair, umbrella case, rusted can,
peach stones, photographs, plastic, wax,
metals, glue, thread
53,7 x 73,2 x 16 cm
Privatsammlung / Private collection

5 O'Clock, 2009
Stoffe, Farbe, Bleistift, Buntstift, Papier, Brot,
Zinn, Fotografien, Korb, bemalte Nussschalen,
Holz, Wolle, Halskette, Ohrring, Weidenkorb,

Klebstoff / Fabrics, paint, pencil, crayon,
paper, bread, tin, photographs, basket, painted
nutshells, wood, wool, necklace, earring,
wicker basket, glue
48 x 75 x 16 cm

39
Setup, 2009
Papier, Kunststoffmatte, getrocknete Früchte,
Tampons, Stoffe, Metalle, Sand, Wachs,
Leder, Fotografien, Plastik, Wolle, Klebstoff,
Sprühfarbe, Zweig, Blatt / Paper, plastic mat,
dried fruit, tampons, fabrics, metals, sand, wax,
leather, photographs, plastics, wool, glue,
spraypaint, twig, leaf
53,7 x 73,2 x 16 cm

40, 41
Not Beyond Repair, 2008
Stoff, pigmentiertes Wachs, Handtuch,
Stofftiere, Draht, Stroh, Plastik, Metallfarbe /
Fabric, pigmented wax, towel, soft toys,
wire, straw, plastic, metal paint
81 x 132 x 80 cm

42
Bundle, 2007
Bauschaum, Draht, Mörtel, Aquarellfarbe,
Ölfarbe / PU foam, wire, mortar, watercolour,
oil paint
34 x 66 x 28 cm
Sender Collection, New York

43
Was soll das, 2008
Bauschaum, Mörtel, Hasendraht, Farbe /
PU foam, mortar, chicken wire, paint
36 x 59 x 91 cm
Sender Collection, New York

44
Porthole, 2009
Beton, Steine, Gips, Pigmente, Glas, Metall,
Kunststoffrohr, Farbflasche, Ohrring /
Concrete, stones, plaster, pigments, glass,
metal, plastic tube, paint-jar, earring
19 x 16 x 18 cm
Privatsammlung / Private collection,
Hong Kong

45
Ensemble, 2008
Holz, Kordel, Stofftiere, Blondierset,
Keramikvase, Klebstoff, Metallringe, Wolle,
Nylontaschen, Metallhaken, Draht, Bast,
Lederbeutel, Goldohrring, Schlüsselanhänger,
Blatt / Wood, string, soft toys, blonde hairdye
packet, ceramic vase, glue, metal rings, wool,
nylon bags, metal hooks, wire, raffia, leather
bumbag, gold earrings, key chain, leaf
158 x 95 x 32 cm
Privatsammlung / Private collection,
New York

46, 47
Flaschengeist, 2008
Stoff, Wolle, Kunststoff, Stahlaufhängung /
Fabric, wool, plastic, steel support
Objekt / Object: 172 x 35 x 45 cm
Stahlaufhängung / Steel support: 45 x Ø 6 cm
Privatsammlung, Köln / Private collection,
Cologne

Flaschengeist, 2008
Stoff, Wolle, Stahlaufhängung / Fabric, wool,
steel support
Objekt / Object: 152 x 35 x 40 cm
Stahlaufhängung / Steel support: 45 x Ø 6 cm
Sammlung Becker, Köln / Cologne

48, 49
Not Ikea, 2009
Rattan, Holz, Acryl, Wolle, Polypropylen, Draht,
Lack, Glas, in Wachs getränkter Stoff, Stoff,
Gips, Seife, Kühlpad, Fotografien, Werbeplakat,
Goldschmuck, Ohrstecker, Haare, Baumrinde,
Sand, Kerngehäuse, Wurstpelle, Brot, Nutella,
Schokoladenpapier, Traubenstrunk, Heiß-
kleber, Kunststoff / Rattan, wood, acrylic, wool,
polypropylene, wire, paint, glass, fabric soaked
in wax, fabric, plaster, soap, cooling pad,
photographs, poster, gold jewellery, earrings,
hair, bark, sand, apple core, sausage skin,
bread, Nutella, chocolate wrappers, grape
stem, hot glue, plastic
240 x 55 x 47 cm
Privatsammlung, Köln / Private collection,
Cologne

50
Knotenbild IV + V, 2009
Fine Art Inkjet Prints kaschiert auf Spanplatte,
Holzrahmen / Fine art ink-jet prints mounted
on chipboard, wood frames
Unikat / Unique copy
2-teilig / 2 parts: 137,2 x 190,5 x 9,4 cm,
170,6 x 99,2 x 9,4 cm
Gesamtmaß / Overall: 170,6 x 190,5 x 18,8 cm

51
Knotenbild II + III, 2009
Fine Art Inkjet Prints kaschiert auf Spanplatte,
Holzrahmen / Fine art ink-jet prints mounted
on chipboard, wood frames
Unikat / Unique copy
2-teilig / 2 parts: 150,2 x 193,4 x 9,4 cm,
190,5 x 137,2 x 9,4 cm
Gesamtmaß / Overall: 190,5 x 193,4 x 18,8 cm
Collection of John Khoury, New York

52
Viss, 2009
Vissflasche, Mörtel, Kunststoff, Legosteine,
Steine, Schiefer, Glas, Postkartenhalter, Vase,
Muschel, Ohrringe, Stöpsel, Sand, Pigmente,
Sockel / Glass cleaner bottle, cement, plastic,
Lego bricks, stone, slate, glass, postcard
holder, vase, shell, earrings, plugs, sand,
pigments, base
Objekt / Object: 27,5 x 29 x 28,5 cm
Sockel / Base: 83,3 x 43,8 x 29,6 cm
Gesamtmaß / Overall: 110,8 x 43,8 x 34,6 cm

53
Bündel, 2009
Bekleidung, Garn / Clothing, yarn
28 x 48 x 37 cm

55
Püppi auf Abwegen, 2009
Schaufensterpuppe, Metallplatte, Mörtel, Erde,
Stofftier, Kehrschaufel, Brotrest, Nutella, Steine,
Schuhkappe, Kunststoff, Plastik, Lippenstift,
Holz, Stickgarn, Gießharz, Jeans, Plastiktüte,
Kastanie, Brötchen, Korken, Nadelkissen,
Nadeln, Haarpackung, Schaumstoff, Muschel,
Stickerei, Porzellan, Schlüsselband, Preisschild,
Gras / Mannequin, metal plate, cement, earth,
soft toy, dustpan, leftover bread, Nutella, stones,
shoe cap, synthetic material, plastic, lipstick,
wood, embroidery, resin, jeans, plastic bag,
chestnut, bread roll, cork, pincushion, pins,
hair wrap, foam, shell, embroidery, porcelain,
lanyard, price tag, grass
123 x 65 x 50,5 cm
Sammlung Becker, Köln / Cologne

56–59
Quelle, 2009
Installation, mixed media
254 x 339 x 177,3 cm

60
www, 2010
Metall, Ast, Kunstast,
Schaufensterpuppenfuß, Kunstharz, Wolle,
Klebstoff / Metal, branch, artificial branch,
mannequin's foot, resin, wool, glue
252 x 98 x 85 cm

61
Alexandria, 2010
Hanfseil, Kunststoffseil, Boje, Rock, Schaukel,
Echthaar, Glas, Gips, Steine, Lampenschirm,
Holz, Haken, Nylon / Hemp rope, synthetic
rope, buoy, skirt, swing, human hair, glass,
plaster, stone, lampshade, wood, hooks,
nylon
322 x 270 x 90 cm

62
Beinahe, 2010
Wachs, Schaufensterpuppenbein, Strumpf-
hose, Ast, Modellhaus (Holz), Schrauben /
Wax, mannequin's leg, tights, branch, toy
house (wood), screws
124 x 52 x 32 cm
Collection Museum Boijmans Van Beuningen,
Rotterdam

63
Installationsansichten / Installation views
Alexandra Bircken, *Blondie*, Kölnischer
Kunstverein, Köln / Cologne, 2010

64, 65
Alexandra Bircken und / and
Thomas Brinkmann
Melanie Vitiligo, 2010
Ski, Echthaar, Heftklammern, Sockel /
Ski, human hair, staples, base
Objekt / Object: 80 x 175 x 10 cm
Sockel / Base: 106 x 70 x 22 cm

65
Alexandra Bircken und / and
Thomas Brinkmann
Pamela Combat, 2010
Ski, Echthaar, Heftklammern / Ski, human
hair, staples
42 x 179 x 12 cm
Collection Museum Boijmans Van Beuningen,
Rotterdam

66
Skiliesel, 2010
Skier, Kupfer, Schrauben, Wachs, Stoff,
Besen, Kunststoffgarn / Skis, copper, screws,
wax, cloth, broom, plastic twine
160 x 40 x 43 cm
Collection Alastair Cookson

67
Fast, 2010
Baumstamm, „Stummer Diener", Stiefel, Gips,
Strumpf, Watte, Leder, Draht, Äste, Wolle,
Stoff, Nadeln, Wachs, T-Shirt, Schrauben /
Tree trunk, "clothes valet", boot, plaster,
stocking, cotton, leather, wire, branches,
wool, fabric, pins, wax, T-shirt, screws
235 x 46 x 65 cm

69
Knut, 2010
Polyesterwattierung, Kunststoffregal,
Klebstoff / Polyester wadding, plastic shelf,
glue
240 x 150 x 120 cm

70
Soulution, 2010
Holz, Beton, Handtuch, Wolle, Draht,
Motorradkette, Ritzel, Drahtkette, Bilder-
rahmen, Strick, Tasche, Farbe, Seife, Tonkrug,
getrocknete Orange / Wood, concrete,
towel, yarn, wire, motorcycle chain, sprocket,
wire chain, picture frame, knit, bag, paint,
soap, clay jug, dried orange
223 x 222 x 64 cm

72
Skin 2, 2010
Polyamid, Elasthan, PVA / Polyamide,
elastane, PVA
126,5 x 136,1 cm
Sammlung Schmidt-Drenhaus, Dresden/
Köln / Cologne

73
Lapsus, 2010
Stoff, Wolle, Mixed Media / Fabric, wool,
mixed media
322,6 x 266,7 x 45,7 cm

74
Take over, 2010
Schaukelpferd, Seil, Farbe, Ball /
Rocking horse, rope, paint, ball
80 x 94 x 41,9 cm

75
Containerland, 2009
Gips, Pappe, Stoff, Toilettenpapierrolle, Lego,
Ohrring, Fotografie, Radiergummi, Wolle, Zwirn,
Kleidung, Plastikbehälter, Wachs, Acryl /
Plaster, cardboard, fabric, toilet roll, lego,
earring, photograph, eraser, yarn, twine,
clothing, plastic containers, wax, acrylic
45 x 40 x 40 cm
Carin und / and James Giddings, New York

76
Ohne Titel, 1991
Kohle, Pastellkreide auf Papier / Charcoal,
pastel on paper
167,6 x 237,5 cm

77
Heart Core, 2011
Holz, Farbe, Leder, Gummi, Metall, Wolle /
Wood, paint, leather, rubber, metal, wool
85 x 55 x 71 cm

78–80
Ohne Titel, 2011
Polypropylenseil / Polypropylene rope
ca. 630 x 860 x 50 cm

81
Ganges, 2011
Stahl, Wolle, Wachs, Draht, Gebetskette,
Zweige, Ast, Latex, Filz, Bügel, getrocknete
Banane, getrockneter Kaktus, Wurzel, Gürtel,
Puppenhaar / Steel, wool, wax, wire, prayer
beads, twigs, branch, latex, felt, coat hanger,
dried banana, dried cactus, root, belt, doll's hair
208,5 x 227 x 81 cm
Sammlung Schmidt-Drenhaus, Dresden/
Köln / Cologne

82
Fabrik, 2011
Polypropylenseil / Polypropylene rope
34 x 126 x 54 cm
Collection of Tristin and Martin Mannion

83
Knochen, 2011
Bronze
18 x 35 x 17 cm
Edition: 5 + 1 AP
Augusta Bariona, Mailand / Milan
Collection of Tristin and Martin Mannion
Gregorio und / and Valeria Napoleone, London
Privatsammlung / Private collection, Düsseldorf
Privatsammlung / Private collection, London

84
Ship II, 2011
Holz, Farbe, Wolle, Metall / Wood, paint,
wool, metal
49 x 40 x 89 cm

85
Womb, 2011
Holz, Metall, Plastik, Stoff, Wolle, verkupferter
Apfel, Seil, Erde / Wood, metal, plastic,
cloth, wool, copper plated apple, rope, earth
180 x 100 x 90 cm

87
Cassius, 2011
Leder, Schaumstoff, Metall / Leather, foam, metal
170 x 81,5 cm
Privatsammlung / Private collection, New York

88
Installationsansichten / Installation views
Alexandra Bircken, *Think of me*, Kimmerich,
New York, 2011

89
8:9, 2011
Verchromter Stahl, Seil / Chrome plated steel,
rope
31,5 cm x Ø 80 cm
Justine und / and Alex Brotmann, Antwerpen /
Antwerp

90
In Mud I Trust, 2011
Stoff, Mörtel, Aluminiumleiste / Fabric, mortar,
aluminium bar
113 x 112,5 cm
Collection of Burt Aaron, Detroit

91
Puli, 2011
Hanfseil / Hemp rope
5-teilig / 5 parts,
je / each ca. 53,4 x 48,3 x 40,6 cm

92
Runner in the Woods, 2011
Holz, Strick, Mörtel, verkupferter Traubenstrunk,
Pigmente, Schrauben / Wood, knit, mortar,
copper plated grape stem, pigments, screws
184 x 170 x 28 cm

93
Spinster, 2011
Holz, Wolle / Wood, wool
176,5 x 59,7 x 55,9 cm

94
Alexandra Bircken und / and
Thomas Brinkmann
Twitter, 2011
Kassettenrecorder, Kassette, Mikrofon,

Stricknadel, gestricktes Kassettenband /
Tape recorder, tape, microphone, knitting
needle, knitted tape
67 x 30,5 x 24,5 cm

95
aHead IV, 2011
Wolle, Stoff, Holz, Gips, Pigmente /
Wool, fabric, wood, plaster, pigments
235 x 26 x 42 cm

aHead III, 2011
Wolle, Stoff, Holz, Gips, Pigmente /
Wool, fabric, wood, plaster, pigments
224 x 28 x 29 cm
Collection of Jill and Peter Kraus, New York

aHead II, 2011
Wolle, Stoff, Holz, Gips, Pigmente /
wool, fabric, wood, plaster, pigments
190,5 x 27,9 x 25,4 cm
Vanessa and Marc Levy Collection,
Antwerpen / Antwerp

aHead I, 2011
Wolle, Leder, Holz, Gips, Pigmente /
Wool, leather, wood, plaster, pigments
241,3 x 57,2 x 73,7 cm

96
Installationsansichten / Installation views
Alexandra Bircken, Studio Voltaire,
London, 2011

97
Abyss, 2011
74 Spiegel / 74 mirrors
613 x 343 cm

98
Birch Field, 2011
Birkenholz, Stoff, Mörtel, Pigment, Schrauben /
Birch wood, cloth, mortar, pigment, screws
168 x 180 x 24 cm
Gregorio und / and Valeria Napoleone, London

99
Extent, 2011
Tuch, Mörtel, Garn / Cloth, mortar, thread
140 x 127 x 10 cm

100/101
Black Skin, 2012
Polyamid, Elasthan, PVA / Polyamide,
elastane, PVA
170 x 220,5 cm
Privatsammlung, Köln / Private collection,
Cologne

102/103
Uknit Bonn, 2012
Stahl, Holz / Steel, wood
150 x 900 cm

104, 105
Installationsansichten / Installation views
Alexandra Bircken, Bonner Kunstverein,
Bonn, 2012

106
Installationsansicht / Installation view
Alexandra Bircken, Hausrat, Kunstverein in
Hamburg, 2012

107
Cagey, 2012
Äste, Weiden, Holz, Stoff, Daunenjacke, Mörtel,
Wolle, Stroh, Seil, Wärmedecke, Bronze,
Rollen, Schrauben / Branches, willow, wood,
fabric, down jacket, mortar, wool, straw, rope,
thermal blanket, bronze, casters, screws
230 x 170 x 170 cm

108, 109
Dummy, 2012
Regenschirm, Pornopuppe, Gips, Pigment,
Ast, Haare, Holzspäne, PVA, Garn / Umbrella,
inflatable doll, plaster, pigment, branch, hair,
wood shavings, PVA, yarn
325 x 160 x 70 cm

110
DNA, 2012
Latex, Äste, Blätter, Holz, Wolle, Schlauch,
Seil, Tonband, Papier, Baumfrucht / Latex,
branches, leaves, wood, wool, hose, rope,
tape, paper, tree fruit
250 x 60 cm

111
Installationsansicht / Installation view
Alexandra Bircken, Hausrat, Kunstverein in
Hamburg, 2012

112
Fadenheim, 2012
Mörtel, Garnrollen, Garnbriefchen, Sprühfarbe / Mortar, cotton reels, thread spool card,
spraypaint
30 x 30 x 23 cm
Privatsammlung / Private collection, Berlin

Koi, 2012
Bronze
20 x 50 x 23 cm
Edition: 5 + 1 AP
Collection Kenneth Akselrod, Antwerpen /
Antwerp
Justine und / and Alex Brotmann, Antwerpen /
Antwerp
Collection Emmy and Danny Lipschutz,
Antwerpen / Antwerp

113
Eddie „The Eagle", 2012
Krümmer, Schlittenkufen, Äste, Mörtelbinden,

Stoff, Schrauben, Seil / Exhaust manifold,
sled runners, branches, cement bandages,
fabric, screws, rope
110 x 90 x 85 cm
Sammlung Haus N, Kiel

114
Installationsansicht / Installation view
Alexandra Bircken, Hausrat, Kunstverein in
Hamburg, 2012

115
Cheri Cheri Lady, 2012
Bügelbrett, Holz, Fell, Latexweste, Ast, Wolle,
Latex, Schrauben / Ironing board, wood,
sheepskin rug, latex waistcoat, branch, wool,
latex, screws
320 x 150 x 60 cm

116, 117
Chariot, 2012
Skateboard, Fahrradrahmen, Schrauben, Äste,
Mörtelbinden, Haare, getrocknetes Gras, Stoff,
Gummi, Draht, Kohle, verkupferte Frucht-
schalen, Kartoffeln, Wachstuch, Latex, Kevlar,
Reisig, Dosendeckel, Feuerwerkskörper,
Schere / Skateboard, bicycle frame, screws,
branches, mortar bandages, hair, dried grass,
fabric, rubber, wire, coal, copper plated fruit
peel, potatoes, waxed cloth, latex, Kevlar,
brushwood, tin can lids, firecracker, scissors
224 x 143 x 171 cm

118
Twins, 2012
Bronze
2-teilig / 2 parts, je / each 25 x 24 x 6 cm
Edition: 5

119
Installationsansichten / Installation views
Alexandra Bircken, Recent Work, Herald St,
London, 2012

120
Twiggy, 2012
Ast, Strumpfhosen, Schraubzwinge, Sockel /
Branch, tights, metal clamp, base
68 x 62 x 38 cm

121
GiMoto, 2012
Leder, Holz, Polsterwatte, Sockel /
Leather, wood, cotton felt stuffing, base
2-teilig / 2 parts: 45 x 14 x 18 cm,
16 x 66 x 25 cm
Gesamtmaß / Overall: 45 x 66 x 32 cm
Wolfgang Tillmans

Alle Arbeiten / All works
Courtesy of BQ, Berlin; Herald St, London;
Kimmerich, New York

Biografie, Bibliografie BIOGRAPHY, BIBLIOGRAPHY

1967
Geboren in Köln / Born in Cologne
Lebt und arbeitet in Köln / Lives and works
in Cologne

1990–1995
Central St. Martins College of Art and Design,
London

EINZELAUSSTELLUNGEN /
SOLO EXHIBITIONS

2013
BQ, Berlin

2012
Recent Work, Herald St, London
Hausrat, Kunstverein in Hamburg
Foyer Bonner Kunstverein, Bonn

2011
Studio Voltaire, London
Think of me, Kimmerich, New York

2010
Storno, BQ, Los Angeles
Blondie, Kölnischer Kunstverein,
Köln / Cologne

2009
Alles muß raus!, BQ, Berlin
Crossings, Herald St, London

2008
Ursula Blickle Stiftung, Kraichtal
Units, Docking Station, Stedelijk Museum,
Amsterdam

2007
Holz, Gladstone Gallery, New York

2006
BQ, Köln / Cologne

2005
Herald St, London

2004
BQ, Köln / Cologne

GRUPPENAUSSTELLUNGEN /
GROUP EXHIBITIONS
(Auswahl / Selection)

2013
Days in Lieu, David Zwirner, London

2012
Neuralgie, Kunstraum Düsseldorf
Made in Germany Zwei, Sprengel Museum
Hannover / Hanover
Everyday Abstract – Abstract Everyday,
James Cohan Gallery, New York
A Disagreeable Object, Sculpture Center, New York

2011
Skulpturales Handeln, Haus der Kunst,
München / Munich
Gesamtkunstwerk: New Art From Germany,
Saatchi Gallery, London
My Beautiful Mongo, Thomas Brambilla,
Bergamo
H x W x D, Wentrup, Berlin
EINS PLUS EINS, M.1 Arthur Boskamp-
Stiftung, Hohenlockstedt
Wash, then dance, Tinderbox, Hamburg
Suspense. Suspended Sculptures, EX3 Centre for
Contemporary Art, Florenz / Florence

2010
Kimmerich, New York

Neues Rheinland. Eine postironische Generation,
Museum Morsbroich, Leverkusen
Folklore?, CRAC Alsace, Altkirch
Undone, Henry Moore Institute, Leeds
Rive droite / Rive gauche, Paris
The Long Dark, Kettle's Yard, Cambridge
SPOT ON 05, Museum Kunstpalast,
Düsseldorf
The same sight slighter, Renwick Gallery,
New York
Feint Art, Kunstverein Freiburg

2009
The Long Dark, The International 3, Manchester;
Hatton Gallery, Newcastle-upon-Tyne
Your Gold Teeth II, Marianne Boesky Gallery,
New York
Arrival Inside, Mary Mary, Glasgow

2008
1st Brussels Biennial, Brüssel / Brussels
Borders, Museum Boijmans Van Beuningen,
Rotterdam
View 14: Hooking up, Mary Boone Gallery,
New York
Martian Museum of Terrestrial Art, Barbican Art
Gallery, London
Paradies und zurück, Sammlung Rheingold in
Schloss Dyck
Anti Baby Pille, Aktualisierungsraum, Hamburg

2007
Unmonumental, New Museum of Contemporary
Art, New York
Hope and Despair, Cell Project Space, London
Um-Kehrungen, Kunstverein Braunschweig
L'Homme nu, Volume 2/3: Paysages visités,
Maison Populaire, Montreuil
L'Homme nu, Volume 1/3: Allures anthropomorphes,
Maison Popoulaire, Montreuil

126

2006

dereconstruction, Gladstone Gallery, New York
Das große Rasenstück. Zeitgenössische Kunst im öffentlichen Raum, Nürnberg / Nuremberg
Kn'-yan, Galerie Christine Mayer, München / Munich

2005

Other People's Projects: Herald St, London, White Columns, New York
Alex Bircken, Mari Eastman, Maaike Schoorel, Maureen Paley Interim Art, London
Us, Herald St, London
fünfmalskulptur, Westfälischer Kunstverein, Münster

KATALOGE / CATALOGUES

Yilmaz Dziewior, Laura Hoptman, Uta Grosenick, eds., *The Art of Tomorrow* (Berlin, 2010), pp. 46–49
Alexandra Bircken, exhib. brochure Museum Kunstpalast (Düsseldorf, 2010)
Nicolaus Schafhausen, Florian Waldvogel, eds., *Alexandra Bircken*, exhib. cat. Ursula Blickle Stiftung, Kraichtal (Cologne, 2008)
Unmonumental, exhib. cat. New Museum, New York (London, 2007)
Alexandra Bircken, *Klötze*, exhib. cat. BQ (Cologne, 2006)
Alex Bircken, exhib. cat. BQ (Cologne, 2004)

REZENSIONEN / REVIEWS
(Auswahl / Selection)

Roberta Smith, "Alexandra Bircken: Think of me", in: *New York Times*, Online Review (September 8th, 2011)
Adelheid Komenda, "Sensibilität und mehrdeutiges Materialspiel", in: *Junge_Kunst*, No. 84 (April, 2010), p. 17

Meike Behm, "Alexandra Bircken", in: *artist kunstmagazin*, No. 84 (2010), pp. 34–39
Elke Buhr, "Alexandra Bircken kombiniert in Köln das Beste aus zwei Welten", in: *Monopol*, No. 6 (Juni, 2010), p. 106
Heidrun Wirth, "Alles hängt am seidenen Faden", in: *Rheinische Rundschau* (April 22nd, 2010), p. 39
Marion Ritter, "Blondiertes Echthaar auf Skiern", in: *Stadtrevue* (May, 2010), p. 60
Mark Prince, "Alexandra Bircken", in: *Frieze*, Online Review (November, 2009)
Sarah Lowndes, "Arrival Inside", in: *Frieze*, Issue 125 (September, 2009), pp. 146–147
Paula Hayes, "Your Gold Teeth II", in: *New York Times* (July 2nd, 2009)
Michelle Cotton, "Alexandra Bircken", in: *Artforum* (February, 2009)
Coline Millard, "Alexandra Bircken", in: *Art in America* (April, 2009)
Karen Rosenberg, "Alexandra Bircken", in: *New York Times* (October 5th, 2007), p. E41
Christabel Steward, "Basel Flush", in: *Tank*, Vol. 4, Issue 10 (2007)
Peter Abs, "Hallo Wände", in: *Spex*, No. 10 (2006), p. 78
Sally O'Reilly, "Alexandra Bircken", in: *Time Out London* (November 16th–23rd, 2005)

Dank THANKS

Wir danken / We would like to thank
den Galerien / the galleries BQ, Berlin, Herald St, London und / and Kimmerich, New York, Friedrich Wolfram Heubach sowie / as well as Stiftung Zukunft NRW.

Bonner Kunstverein dankt / would like to thank
Meyer-Köring für die Unterstützung der Ausstellung / for the support of the exhibition.

Kunstverein in Hamburg dankt / would like to thank
den Leihgebern der Ausstellung / the lenders for the exhibition, Westag & Getalit AG, Jana Joppe und / and Isaac & Lily Waldvogel.

Alexandra Bircken dankt / would like to thank
Samara Aster, Walter Asmuth, Jörn Bötnagel, Herbert und / and Irmgard Bircken, Thomas Brinkmann, Michelle Cotton, Patrizia Dander, Anja Dorn, Fa. Eiting, Karla und / and Alexander Faridi, Westag & Getalit AG, Monika Gsella, Anna Grande, Annette Hans, Fritz Heubach, Andreas Hoppmann, Lutz Huelle, Kathrin Jentjens, Dennis Kimmerich, Brigitte Kölle, Ash L'ange, Julienne Lorz, Valeria und / and Gregorio Napoleone, Silke Otto-Knapp, Yvonne Quirmbach, Thomas Rosenbaum und / and Team, Lothar Schnepf, Martin Schweitzer, Joe Scotland, Michael Stockhausen, Bruni und / and Wolfgang Strobel, Wolfgang Tillmans, Claudia und / and Kurt von Storch, Christina Végh, Nicky Verber, Florian Waldvogel und / and Prof. Louise Wilson.

Diese Publikation erscheint anlässlich der Ausstellungen *Alexandra Bircken* im Bonner Kunstverein, 17. April – 25. November 2012 und *Alexandra Bircken: Hausrat* im Kunstverein in Hamburg, 12. Mai – 2. September 2012. This book is being published on the occasion of the exhibitions *Alexandra Bircken* at Bonner Kunstverein, April 17th – November 25th, 2012 and *Alexandra Bircken: Hausrat* at Kunstverein in Hamburg, May 12th – September 2nd, 2012.

BONNER KUNSTVEREIN

Hochstadenring 22, D–53119 Bonn
T: +49 (0)228 693936
F: +49 (0)228 695589
kontakt@bonner-kunstverein.de
www.bonner-kunstverein.de

Direktorin / Director
Christina Végh
Kuratorin / Curator
Fanny Gonella
Volontär / Junior Curator
Michael Stockhausen
Sekretariat / Office
Bodo Hoffmann, Christine Hütten, Stella Weidner
Mitgliederbetreuung / Member Support
Gerda Schuwirth
Technik / Technical Support
Benjamin Juran, Dirk Ufermann
Artothek
Elisabeth Wynhoff

Vorstand / Board
Dr. Nicolai Besgen (Schriftführer / Secretary), Prof. Henning Boecker (1. Vorsitzender / Chairman), Prof. Anne-Marie Bonnet (2. Vorsitzende / Vice-Chairwoman), Dr. Alexander Braun, Gisela Clement, Dipl.-Kfm. Christoph Kurpiers (Schatzmeister / Treasurer), Michael Plössner, Dr. Anke Schierholz, Dr. Manfred von Seggern, Linde Trottenberg, Stefan Weidle

Der Kunstverein wird gefördert von / The Kunstverein is funded by Stadt Bonn.

**FREUDE.
JOY.
JOIE.
BONN.**

DER KUNSTVEREIN, SEIT 1817.

Kunstverein in Hamburg e.V.
Klosterwall 23, D–20095 Hamburg
T. +49 (0)40 322157
F. +49 (0)40 322159
hamburg@kunstverein.de
www.kunstverein.de

Direktor / Director
Florian Waldvogel
Kuratoren / Curators
Annette Hans, Martijn van Dijk
*Presse und Öffentlichkeitsarbeit /
Press and Public Relations*
Beate Anspach
Projektleitung / Project Management
Corinna Koch
Kuratorische Assistenz / Curatorial Assistant
Marc Böhnke
Mitgliederbetreuung / Member Support
Brigitte Skerra
Technische Leitung / Technical Director
Robert Görß
Buchhaltung / Administration
Gesche Früchtenicht

Vorstand / Board
Katharina Bittel, Harald Falckenberg (Vorsitzender / Chairman), Mathias Güntner, Tilman Kriesel, Ernst Josef Pauw, Bernhard Prinz, Nora Sdun, Christoph Seibt, Andras Siebold

Der Kunstverein wird gefördert von / The Kunstverein is funded by Kulturbehörde der Freien und Hansestadt Hamburg.

Hamburg | Kulturbehörde

PUBLIKATION / PUBLICATION

Herausgeber / Editor
Christina Végh, Florian Waldvogel
Gestaltung / Graphic Design
Yvonne Quirmbach, Berlin
Texte / Texts
Annette Hans, Friedrich Wolfram Heubach, Christina Végh
Übersetzungen / Translations
Timothy Connell (Hans, Végh),
James Gussen (Heubach)

Fotonachweis / Photo Credits
Alexandra Bircken (41), Alex Delfanne, London (42, 45), Fred Dott, Hamburg (73, 77–83, 106–115), Andy Keate, London (35–40, 44, 75, 84, 96–99, 116–121), Roman März, Berlin (50–59), Jacopo Menzani (70), Thomas Müller, New York (87–95), Lothar Schnepf, Köln / Cologne (46–49, 60–62, 65–69, 85, 100/101), Simon Vogel, Köln / Cologne (63, 64, 102–105), Joshua White, Los Angeles (72, 74, 76)

Lithografie / Lithography
max-color, Berlin
Druck / Print
DZA Druckerei zu Altenburg GmbH

Erschienen im / Published by
Verlag der Buchhandlung Walther König, Köln
Ehrenstr. 4, D–50672 Köln
T: +49 (0)221 2059653
F: +49 (0)221 2059660
verlag@buchhandlung-walther-koenig.de

Bibliografische Information der Deutschen Nationalbibliothek
Die Deutsche Nationalbibliothek verzeichnet diese Publikation in der Deutschen National-bibliografie; detaillierte bibliografische Daten sind über http://dnb.d-nb.de abrufbar.

© 2013
Alexandra Bircken; Bonner Kunstverein; Kunstverein in Hamburg e.V.; die Fotografen / the photographers; die Autoren / the authors und / and Verlag der Buchhandlung Walther König, Köln / Cologne

Vertrieb / Distribution
Schweiz / Switzerland
AVA Verlagsauslieferungen AG
Centralweg 16, CH–8910 Affoltern a.A.
T: +41 (44) 7624260
F: +41 (44) 7624210
verlagsservice@ava.ch

Großbritannien & Irland / UK & Eire
Cornerhouse Publications
70 Oxford Street, GB–Manchester M1 5NH
T: +44 (0)161 2001503
F: +44 (0)161 2001504
publications@cornerhouse.org

Außerhalb Europas / Outside Europe
D.A.P. / Distributed Art Publishers, Inc.
155 6th Avenue, 2nd Floor,
USA–New York, NY 10013
T: +1 (0) 212 627 1999
F: +1 (0) 212 627 9484
eleshowitz@dapinc.com

ISBN 978-3-86335-313-1

Printed in Germany

Diese Publikation wird ermöglicht durch die großzügige Unterstützung der / This publication is made possible by the generous support of **Stiftung Zukunft NRW**.